Sex . . .
God's Truth

ELLEL MINISTRIES
THE TRUTH AND FREEDOM SERIES

Sex ...
God's Truth

Jill Southern

Sovereign World

Sovereign World Ltd
PO Box 784
Ellel
Lancaster LA1 9DA
England

ISBN 978 1 85240 452 9

Cover design by Andy Taylor, Ellel Ministries
Typeset by CRB Associates, Reepham, Norfolk
Printed in Malta

Contents

About the Author

From the age of fourteen when she became a Christian, Jill knew that God had a destiny and purpose for her life. Despite success in her career in Sales and Marketing with Thorn EMI in London and a happy marriage to Ron, she had a major problem with claustrophobic fear. This led her to attend the Ellel Ministries' conference "The Battle Belongs to the Lord" in June 1990 where she was powerfully set free.

Soon after God very clearly spoke to Jill from 1 Kings 19 about the call of God on Elisha who left his job to follow the God of Elijah. She left Thorn EMI in December 1992 and in January 1993 attended the second nine-week school run by Ellel Ministries at Glyndley Manor, Eastbourne.

In March 1994, when a local school estate called Pierrepont went on the market, God told Jill to take Peter Horrobin to see it and he sensed that this should be the International Training Center for Ellel. When the thirty-five-acre estate was purchased in February 1995 Jill became the Center Director. That whole story is the subject for another book! Jill says it has been the best ten years of her life and a mighty life-changing adventure with God. God has called her to teach kingdom truth and pray the application of it into others' lives starting with her own! *Sex . . . God's Truth* is her first book.

Foreword

We live in a world that is frequently dominated by images and talk of sex and sexuality – almost universally in a way that is ungodly and unhealthy! Sex is often used to attract and sell – everything from ice-cream to motor cars. The pressures on children of school age to experiment with different sexual relationships and orientations leave most young people with a relationship history which is a million miles from what God intended.

Jill writes on this very sensitive subject with passionate enthusiasm. Her desire to help people be healed from the consequences of their sexual past and to set godly standards for their future comes through every chapter. This book is a gold-mine of straightforward information and teaching, told in a way that is not only very real but also very scriptural and inspirational.

In our many years of ministry we have seen that when people receive healing from the consequences of their past relationships, the godly benefits are very far-reaching, releasing the life-transforming power of God into their lives. I believe this book will meet a deep need in many people's lives.

Peter Horrobin
International Director of Ellel Ministries

Let's Talk about Sex

It is very easy for us to believe that we know everything there is to know about sex. After all it has a very high profile all around us, on television, in magazines and in advertising. Most of us consider we have been "in the know" for most of our lives!

Perishing for lack of knowledge

As I have traveled to many countries in the world, teaching God's truth about sex and sexuality, it has become increasingly clear to me that even God's people tend to know only the biological facts about sex and to be influenced by the attitudes towards it in the culture around them.

The trouble with allowing the world to shape our values and opinions is that it can fall a long way short of God's truth. The world itself is liable to be deceived in many ways. From the lips of Jesus we learn that "the prince of this world" is Satan and that there is a time for him to be driven out (John 12:31; 14:30). Satan, according to Jesus, is the father of lies (John 8:44).

The ignorance I find amongst God's people frequently brings home to me the reality and truth of the words spoken by the prophet Hosea, *"my people are destroyed from lack of knowledge"* (Hosea 4:6). The Word of God is infallible and totally inspired by the Holy Spirit and ought to be our plumbline for all matters of Christian faith and behavior. The whole truth about sex and sexuality is not being taught in many churches. As Christian believers we need to learn about sex from God's viewpoint or we will have a very inadequate picture.

Whilst the Church's standards in sexual matters may be higher than those of the world they are often still nowhere near God's standards. Scripture says that God's Word *"is eternal"* (Psalm 119:89) and that with God *"there is no variation or shadow of turning"* (James 1:17 NKJV). As the world's standards sink, the Church's standards can also spiral in a downward direction. Maybe through embarrassment, the truth of God in this area is not taught clearly and in sufficient detail for people to understand.

Sexual sin seems to be rampant in the world around us – fornication, adultery, same-sex relationships. Such behavior is sin but is treated as being the "norm." It is included in the TV soaps and enters into every aspect of life today. It appears in advertising for cars, holidays and almost anything. Sadly there is scarcely any mention of sex in the context of God's truth. Sometimes it seems as if Satan has hijacked sex but we should remember that sex was *God's* idea in the first place.

The pinnacle of God's creation

To understand God's plan for our sexuality let us consider human life itself. We are not a chance product of evolution but a very special creation of God. We were created by Almighty God, who always was, is and always will be. As it says in Colossians 1:16–17, referring to the Lord Jesus Christ,

> *For by him all things were created: things in heaven and on earth, visible and invisible, whether thrones or powers or rulers or authorities; all things were created by him and for him. He is before all things, and in him all things hold together.*

You were created by God in accordance with His plans and purpose (including your sexuality), and you are the pinnacle of

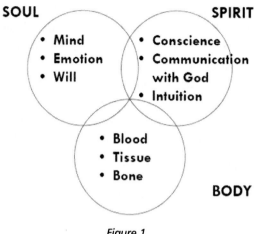

SOUL   SPIRIT

* Mind   * Conscience
* Emotion   * Communication
* Will   with God
                    * Intuition

        * Blood
        * Tissue
        * Bone
                              BODY

Figure 1

His creation. You are made in His image, as a spiritual being, with a soul, in a body (see figure 1). This is clear from passages in the Bible such as 1 Thessalonians 5:23 which says, *"May your whole spirit, soul and body be kept blameless at the coming of our Lord Jesus Christ."*

The body is the part of us that is clearly seen and can be touched. It contains various constituents such as our bone structure, our internal organs or tissue, our skin and our blood. Our bodies also outwardly reflect our God-given sexual identity.

Our soul is invisible and not so easily understood. It contains three parts: the emotions with which we feel, the mind with which we think and process information, and the will with which decisions and choices are made.

Our human spirit is more mysterious and can be said to contain the conscience, creativity and our communication path with God. The conscience enables us to know right and wrong. Creativity, a quality which is characteristic of human beings, is a reflection of God as the Creator. We are made in His image, and so we have the capacity to be creative. The communication path with God in the human spirit enables us to know Him through hearing His voice, through worship and through prayer.

Intuitively we can know something that we have no knowledge of with the mind, or intellect, and which is outside our experience. For example, we may go somewhere we have never been before and for some reason feel uncomfortable and want to leave. We don't know why. It is an impression that we receive in our spirit. The human spirit can act like an early warning radar system from God. Rationalizing this prompting with the mind can block it and stop God from reaching us effectively.

God chose to create us all as either male or female. We read this in Genesis 1:27, a scripture quoted by Jesus when He said,

> *"Haven't you read ... that at the beginning the Creator 'made them male and female ... '?"*
>
> (Matthew 19:4)

Human sexuality must firstly be understood within the terms of God's original plan. Jesus goes on to say (quoting Genesis 2:24),

> *" 'For this reason a man will leave his father and mother and be united to his wife, and the two shall become one flesh.' So they are no longer two, but one."*

During sexual intercourse a man and his wife, two distinct individuals, become one.

Although sex is a joining together of their two bodies, it actually involves a union of every part of them. This is not just temporary. This "one flesh" bonding means a link of spirit, soul and body. Other parts of the Bible refer to this unity. In Malachi 2:14 God challenges the men of Israel about the way they are treating *"the wife of* [their] *youth,"* whom he also describes as *"the wife of* [their] *marriage covenant."* He then asks this question, *"Has not the LORD made them one? In flesh and spirit they are his"* (Malachi 2:15).

Sexual intercourse, for us as human beings, should be one of the highest acts our body, soul and spirit are capable of and should involve all that we are at the very deepest level. Sexuality is extremely powerful and meant to be far more than a biological need or urge. Sex is a most beautiful gift of God, but it is intended by Him to be expressed within the marriage covenant.

God's plan for sex

In the beginning God ordained that sex in the relationship of marriage should bring glory and honor to Him, as the Creator. He was very pleased with all that He had made. As we continue to bring pleasure to God in fulfilling His original plan for sexual relationship and intimacy within the covenant of marriage we are bringing glory and honor to Him. This can be likened to worship. Whenever we honor or worship God and are obedient to His will in our lives it means God can pour out His blessing upon us.

A wider concept of worship

Perhaps we need to expand our view of what the word "worship" means. If we think of worship as singing songs to God or something we do in a church setting, we are failing to grasp the whole story. Jesus said,

> *"God is Spirit, and those who worship Him must worship in spirit and truth."*
>
> (John 4:24 NKJV)

True worship touches the heart of God. It is what brings Him joy and blessing.

The psalmist tells us that God inhabits the praises of His people (Psalm 22:3 NKJV) and as we praise Him, He in return blesses us. We are in a relationship of love with Him. Through worship there is, therefore, an intermingling of God's Spirit and our spirit. Worship goes up to God and blessing comes down to man, through which we are nurtured and strengthened in our spirit. Life is imparted to our spirit.

To return to God's plan for sex, I believe that, in the same way that God's Spirit and ours are joined together in worship, the spirits of a married couple experiencing sexual intercourse touch each other and there is a mutual exchange of something intangible that is very precious and very deep. This is also very pleasing to God, bringing joy to His heart in the same way as a conscious act of worship does (see figure 2).

In the illustration you will notice a line joining husband and wife. This line symbolizes the godly soul-tie that is established between them as they become "one." When we consider marriage, God intended the two should become one, through sexual intercourse, and when this happens a godly soul-tie is established which enables an intermingling of the two people to take place.

Recently I was taking a photograph at a sixtieth wedding anniversary and I thought, "They even look like each other!" Not surprising really when you consider they have been intermingling together for sixty years. Even when a husband and wife are geographically separated, something intangible is still joining them together.

The marriage union should be a free-will choice and is not only intended to be very exciting emotionally but also for there to be a mental oneness and a spiritual joining. Through this act of love, the spirit is nurtured and built up and mutual comfort and support is experienced. There is the touching of spirits and a deep sense of belonging and security. This is why Paul says that married couples should not withhold intercourse from each other (1 Corinthians 7:5).

Sexual intercourse in marriage is not just about reproduction. It is intended by God that sex continues throughout the marriage because through it there is a mutual exchange of love, support and comfort and a flow of God's blessing. This keeps the marriage strong and maintains the special, unique and exclusive bonding that God wants for a married couple.

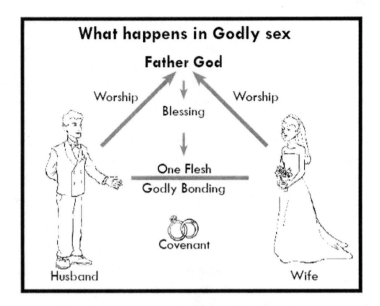

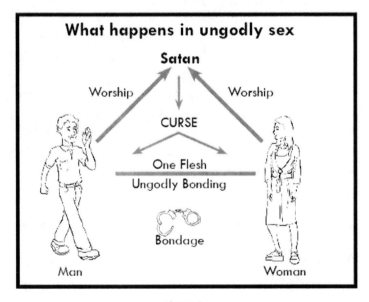

Figure 2

Summary

I have looked at God's plan for sex and how it has become so little understood and accepted by the world today and sometimes sadly even within the Church. God's original plan was that sex should be reserved for the security of a marriage relationship, and yet it seems that Satan has been able to hijack this plan in much of society. As the world's standards have sunk lower and lower and sexual sin has become so widespread, it might cause us to despair that the younger generation would ever be able to stand up against the tremendous peer pressure they face today. It is encouraging to know that not all young people are being squeezed into conforming to the mould of the world.

Pam Stenzel in her book *Sex Has a Price Tag*[1] describes how a Christian girl made a promise to God to keep herself pure for her husband until their marriage. One day in the sixth form the usual boasting and bragging about sexual conquests was going on and her fellow students turned to her and asked: "How many boys have you been with?" "None," she replied. Her peer group fell about laughing. "You're not serious? Is there something wrong with you? Are you frigid or something?" Her commendable reply was: "Any day I want to, I can be like you – but you can never be like me! I am keeping myself for my husband and that is the most important gift that I can give him – myself as a virgin on my wedding day." The laughing stopped and there was no answer from them in response to that.

In the next chapter we will look at the importance of the covenant of marriage and the implications that it has for a couple as they enter into this special God-ordained relationship.

Note _____

1. Zondervan, 2003.

Why Marry?

In this modern age many couples have chosen to live together without going through a marriage ceremony. By making this decision, they are choosing to go outside of God's plan and are forfeiting the blessings that could be theirs. In this chapter I want to look at the importance of the marriage covenant and godly order within the family relationship.

God has made a covenant with His people

The Old Testament records that God entered into a solemn covenant with the Jewish race. Likewise, Christian believers are in a covenant love relationship with God through the shed blood of Jesus Christ. Jesus described this as the new covenant:

> While they were eating, Jesus took bread, gave thanks and broke it, and gave it to his disciples, saying, "Take it; this is my body." Then he took the cup, gave thanks and offered it to them, and they all drank from it. "This is my blood of the covenant, which is poured out for many," he said to them.
>
> (Mark 14:22–24)

This, of course, is what the service of Holy Communion is about. It is remembering that the death of Jesus was necessary before we could enter into that covenant relationship. This covenant was initiated by God, as the stronger party, with man as the weaker party. God initiates covenant with man through Jesus. The Scriptures tell us that Jesus *"steadfastly set His face to go to Jerusalem"* (Luke 9:51 NKJV). In Hebrews 12:2 we discover why He was prepared to do so: *"for the joy that was set before Him* [He] *endured the cross, despising the shame"* (Hebrews 12:2 NKJV). You and I, as Christian believers, are part of that joy. The covenant that we have with God is an exclusive covenant and is our most precious relationship of all.

God says,

> *"I am the LORD your God ... You shall have no other gods before me."*
>
> (Exodus 20:2, 3)

He wants us to forsake all other gods and cling only to Him, the one true God. I am so glad that God is jealous over our love. God desires that our heart attitude toward Him be that summarized in the words of the song by William J. Reynolds:

> I have decided to follow Jesus ...
> The world behind me, the cross before me ...
> Though none go with me, I still will follow ...
> No turning back!
> No turning back![1]

God doesn't want to share us with any false god. He wants all of our love and all of our worship. God will never break His covenant with us. He tells us, *"I will never leave you nor forsake you"* (Hebrews 13:5 NKJV) and *"no one can snatch them out of my Father's hand"* (John 10:29).

God's perfect will for men and women is for them to enter into covenant with Him. God always intended that our primary relationship should be with Him. We were created with a God-shaped hole that knows no satisfaction outside of Him.

Figure 3

Through the work of Jesus on the cross, we are reconciled to the Father. Our "vertical" relationship with God is to be one of reconciliation, harmony and peace through Jesus Christ, where we receive His love (see figure 3).

God's will is for us to relate to Him as the source of all things. He is to come first in our lives:

> *Love the LORD your God with all your heart and with all your*
> *soul and with all your strength.*
>
> (Deuteronomy 6:5)

God's ideal plan is that mature adults are able to be complete in Him and find their needs for love (security, significance and self-worth) being met first of all by Him.

However, God has also planned for each human being to be in relationship with others and for those relationships to be a great blessing. These "horizontal" relationships should flow out of the one we have with God. We need to be able to fully receive His love into our hearts and then, having received from

God, be able to be a "giver" in human relationships not just a "taker." I believe that unless our relationship with God is right, none of our other relationships will be right.

The marriage covenant

For married people their partner should be their best friend. Their marriage should be their foremost human relationship, where there is mutual sharing of the whole of their lives together.

Marriage is intended by God to be a covenant relationship. In the New Testament Jesus is likened to a bridegroom and the Church of Christ to a bride. The marriage covenant is intended to reflect God's covenant with His people. Marriage is one of God's most beautiful and precious gifts to mankind but the enemy is for ever seeking to distort and spoil that gift.

There are three parts to the marriage covenant. The first part is **the making of the vows**. For a sexual relationship to be under God's blessing, these vows must be made first before the consummation of a marriage takes place. The second part is the **leaving and cleaving**. The third part is **consummation through sexual intercourse**. The marriage is then complete and is meant to be a permanent and exclusive relationship until death, with sexual intercourse continuing to take place throughout the marriage.

Whenever we read of covenant in the Bible we also read of sacrifice and the shedding of blood because covenant represents a final and irrevocable commitment in relationship. Derek Prince, in his book *The Marriage Covenant*, writes:

> The sacrifice upon which the covenant of Christian marriage is based is the death of Jesus Christ on our behalf.

He goes on to say,

> First a life is laid down. Each lays down his life for the other. Each must say, "Now I am no longer living for

myself." This is true because in our single days we could mostly please ourselves, now we cannot, because we have to consider the need of our marriage partner as a priority.[2]

It is interesting to me that, in the Old Testament, covenants were sealed by the shedding of blood. We could regard the covenant of marriage as being sealed with the shedding of blood at the consummation by sexual intercourse. In earlier times in the Jewish culture, after consummation of the marriage, the parents of the bride would show the sheets off the bed, stained with blood, to demonstrate that their daughter was a virgin and also that the marriage had been consummated. The technical test for a virgin was that her hymen had not been previously broken and the first intercourse penetrated the hymen and shed blood. Additionally non-consummation of the marriage was a legal reason for the marriage to be annulled.

The biblical basis for marriage being a covenant is found throughout Scripture but probably best evidenced by Malachi 2:14:

> *It is because the LORD is acting as a witness between you and the wife of your youth, because you have broken faith with her, though she is your partner, the wife of your marriage covenant.*

Legal relationship

There is also a need to be legally married according to the laws of the country in which we live. It is so important as Christians that we *"render ... to Caesar the things that are Caesar's, and to God the things that are God's"* (Matthew 22:21 NKJV). We should have a legal marriage certificate, so that the world does not look on us as "living in sin" and so that we are good witnesses to Jesus Christ in the community in which we live. We are called to be salt and light in the world (Matthew 5:13–14).

I prayed with a couple who told me that they did not have a marriage certificate but had simply made their vows together before God and started living as husband and wife. Two things are wrong with that:

- not rendering to Caesar the things that are Caesar's
- not making the covenant of marriage before witnesses.

I suggested that they repent and fix a proper wedding date and separate sexually until that time. Rather than just going through the legal formalities, I also recommended that they should ask their pastor if he would conduct a service before Christian witnesses.

Recently some Christian friends went to a registry office to obtain their legal marriage certificate. They told me they asked the very nice lady in the registry office if they could have a prayer to God and she told them very clearly, "Absolutely not – no prayers to any God allowed!" To their question, "Could we just have this hymn/song then?" the response was, "Absolutely no hymns!" I believe there is a spirit behind this, a spirit of secular humanism, the spirit of the age, an Anti-Christ spirit.

> We wrestle not against flesh and blood, but against princip-
> alities, against powers ...
>
> (Ephesians 6:12 KJV)

Registry office weddings fulfill the law alone and actually are humanistic. They do not make a covenant of marriage before God. As we move into the last days we need to be clear in our teaching to believers that, for the Christian, both the legal requirement and the covenant before God should be fulfilled.

Can't afford to get married!

While speaking with a really earnest Christian couple at the end of one of my teaching sessions on sex and sexuality, I challenged them about the fact that they were living together. "Why are you doing it?" I asked them. "Well, actually," they replied, "we can't afford the wedding!" For this couple, the inability to follow the world's pattern of spending thousands of pounds on a lavish wedding and the fear of what others might think led them to justify their living together in an ungodly relationship. Worldly pressures can be a challenge to Christians, but do we have to submit to them? At Ellel Ministries' centers we often find our full-time workers fall in love and want to be married! Our centers are not usually solemnized for weddings so they arrange to be legally married at a registry office, but at this point they do not consummate the marriage or move in to live together. The next day we hold the marriage service when they make their covenant before God, friends and family. We are making a declaration into the heavenly realm and what we speak out here in the earthly realm has a correlation in the heavenly realm.

The wedding can be a simple affair. Someone does the flowers; maybe the dress is borrowed. The service is always very meaningful. Often the couple write their own vows which will include leaving their birth parents and cleaving to each other alone and that this will be until death parts them. Photos and a celebration party follow and they leave for a honeymoon together.

This does not need to cost very much but is the best possible "send off" into married life and very memorable for the bride and bridegroom who consummate their marriage after the covenant has been made. Usually at the wedding service, the couple exchange rings. We anoint the rings with oil and pray over them. The rings symbolize the marriage. We bless the rings in Jesus' name and pray for their unending love for each other.

Derek Prince says,

> Israel had come to view marriage as a relationship for which they might set their own standards – one which they were free to initiate or terminate on their own terms. God reminds them however that He views marriage quite differently. According to His unchanging purposes marriage is a covenant. This is the secret which alone

ensures the success of the marriage relationship. Once this secret is forgotten or ignored, marriage must inevitably lose its sanctity and thereby also its strength and stability. Much of what we see in contemporary civilisation is closely paralleled to the condition of Israel in Malachi's day and the root cause is the same – a wrong view of marriage.[3]

Marriage is a covenant not a contract

In a marriage everything the husband has belongs to the wife, and vice versa, and each holds nothing back from the other. God's Word knows nothing of the pre-nuptial agreements many well-known personalities enter into, which set down legally binding arrangements over what happens to their personal wealth and possessions if the marriage is terminated by divorce.

God's Word makes no provision for such marriage covenants, because marriage is a covenant. Christian marriage is a relationship between husband and wife with the Lord Jesus Christ at the center. Ecclesiastes 4:12 tells us that *"A cord of three strands is not quickly broken."* Worldly marriage contracts are about what I can get from this relationship, how I can protect myself and my possessions. Covenant is about what I can bring into this relationship, how I can best give of myself. A contract can be ended but God intended the marriage covenant to be totally binding until the death of one of the parties. Paul writes,

> *by law a married woman is bound to her husband as long as he is alive, but if her husband dies, she is released from the law of marriage.*
>
> (Romans 7:2)

The wedding ceremony, in which solemn promises or vows are made before God, should take place in the presence of witnesses.

The following story illustrates a wedding ceremony in which God is honored above all. I shall call this fictitious young couple James and Amanda.

Preparation for marriage

James and Amanda met at the local church where they were both in the youth group. They became Christians, Amanda as a result of being brought up in a Christian home and James as a result of an evangelical mission. Jesus Christ was Lord of their lives.

James and Amanda were deeply in love and chose to go to different universities to make sure their love was of the lasting kind. James asked Amanda to marry him and they managed to secure jobs and to save some money for their life together. They decided to keep themselves pure for their wedding night. At times this was hard but James told Amanda: "This is the most precious wedding gift that I can give to you. I give you myself without any previous sexual partners. I can only give that to one person and I want to give that to you as my wife."

Amanda believed this to be important too but could hardly wait for the wedding to come. Their pastor took them through eight weeks of pre-marriage counseling where they looked at important issues such as whether they were realistic about the demands of marriage, and whether they could accept each other's personalities, habits and faults. They discussed such questions as:

- Were they able to share their feelings and ideas and discuss their differences?
- Did they mostly agree on big decisions and financial matters?
- Did they share the same spiritual values?
- Did they agree on the number of children they wanted and the sharing of responsibilities?

- Were they comfortable discussing sexual issues together?
- Did they have a good relationship with each other's families and each other's friends?
- Were they emotionally close to each other?
- Did they have shared interests and enjoy time together?

Some of these issues made them think hard about exactly what was involved in Christian marriage but they ended up convinced more than ever that they wanted to share the rest of their lives together.

Amanda and her mother planned the wedding for months. It was not going to be a hugely extravagant affair but a very meaningful celebration of their marriage covenant.

The marriage vows

After the opening hymn, the pastor prayed and then led them in their wedding vows. These were witnessed by family, friends and many people from the church. James and Amanda made their covenant of marriage before God and the congregation.

"I take you, Amanda," said James, "to be my lawful wedded wife, to have and to hold from this day forward, for better, for worse, for richer, for poorer, in sickness and in health, forsaking all others and cleaving always only to you. I give you my solemn vow and ask God to be my witness and my helper till death parts us."

Amanda replied, "I take you, James, to be my lawful wedded husband, to have and to hold from this day forward, for better, for worse, for richer, for poorer, in sickness and in health, forsaking all others and cleaving always only to you. I will love and obey you. I give you my solemn vow and ask God to be my witness and my helper till death parts us."

They exchanged rings and after the pastor had blessed them, they each said to the other: "I give you this ring as a token and memorial of our never-ending love and our marriage."

Leaving and cleaving

Therefore shall a man leave his father and his mother, and shall cleave unto his wife: and they shall be one flesh.

(Genesis 2:24 KJV; cf. Ephesians 5:31)

In the traditional British wedding service the question is asked: "Who will give this woman to be wed?" Usually the father of the bride replies, "I will." However, it is imperative that both sets of parents agree to the release of their child, physically, emotionally and spiritually. The wedding signals the commencement of a new family unit and without proper leaving, cleaving rarely happens.

Mother-in-law jokes probably stem from the fact that mothers often find it very difficult to fully release their "adult children" into their marriages and step back from interfering between the new husband and wife, allowing them to make their own mistakes and to make all their own decisions.

Children are a gift from the Lord and are the fruit of a marriage. Our children are not ours alone: they belong to God and are entrusted to us by Him to bring them up in the *"nurture and admonition of the Lord"* (Ephesians 6:4 KJV). This means that we should teach and train them in the things of God, praying that they themselves will become Christians and repent of their own sins and turn to Him.

By the time the bride and bridegroom come to be married, the parents must consider their job in bringing them up as completed. The parents need to release their adult child into the new family unit, which begins on their wedding day. In the wedding ceremony it is better that both sets of parents stand at the front and speak out their willingness to release their adult child and be willing to step back from the number one place they used to hold in their child's life.

The husband is now the spiritual and emotional cover for his wife and this is no longer to be her parents' role. The husband is to be the number one person in her life and it should no longer be her mother or father. In some cultures it is also important to say that the wife cannot accept her mother-in-law as the number one person in her life either.

In the event of the bride or groom being a twin or having previously had an extremely close relationship with a sister or brother, there may also be a need to speak out a complete releasing of old forms of family relationship in order that the marriage has the place of priority.

Many marriages flounder because of a misunderstanding of the truth behind leaving and cleaving. This may be the unwillingness of one or both of the parents to cut the apron strings and release their children, or it may be the unwillingness of the new marriage partner to leave, spiritually and emotionally. This pollutes the marriage covenant.

In Ellel Ministries, we vigorously support Christian marriage and have prayed with people who have told us that their marriage had irretrievably broken down only to see God transform it into something far better than ever before.

Consequences of not leaving

Adam and Debbie came for help because Debbie was continually upset by the behavior of Adam's mother. Adam was an only child and his father had died before he was married to Debbie. Adam's mother had always seemed to be aloof from Debbie, preferring to see her son on his own whenever possible. Debbie had worked hard at trying to win her over but to no avail. They had three children and, as the years had gone by, the relationship between Debbie and her mother-in-law had worsened.

Finally things came to a head when Adam was planning to take Debbie out for a special meal on their wedding anniversary. The children were being looked after by a neighbor and Debbie was putting on her best dress when the phone rang and Adam answered it. It was his mother in quite a state saying he must come over straight away as she had a water leak under the sink and she was already starting an asthma attack because of the stress of it.

Adam turned to Debbie, "I'm sorry, love, but you know my mother has a weak heart and I wouldn't want anything to happen to her and I'd never relax eating the meal knowing she was in need."

Adam went, leaving Debbie in tears and also angry because she knew mother was still pulling his strings and continued to interfere in the marriage. She could never rely on anything as definite because Adam's mother could interrupt their plans at any time. When Adam finally returned, wet and tired, it was too late to go out and so instead they had an enormous row. "You should have told your mother to get a plumber!" screamed Debbie. "You should feel more compassion for my old widowed mother!" yelled back Adam.

As they told their story, we shared with them about leaving and cleaving. We prayed with them and Adam agreed not to come under his mother's domination, manipulation and control. He was able to realize how, after all these years, he could still relegate Debbie to the number two position and how this was interfering in the marriage. It took a while but as he really started to take up his rightful headship, put his wife first and chose not to come under his mother's control, the marriage came into godly order. Both became much happier and more secure in the marriage.

Whenever we pray for marriages in trouble, we look at the foundations. Leaving and cleaving is one of the critical foundations that need to be in godly order if we want to see happy and sustained Christian marriages.

Consummation through sexual intercourse

We have been looking at the three parts of the marriage covenant, and now we come to the final part which is the consummation through sexual intercourse. When the bodily union of sexual intercourse takes place for the first time, the marriage is said to be consummated. Additionally it is right that there is a fulfilling of the civil laws regarding marriage. Non-consummation is legal grounds to have the marriage annulled or for it to end in divorce.

Sexual relations are expected to continue throughout the marriage. As the apostle Paul says in 1 Corinthians 7:2–5,

> *But since there is so much immorality, each man should have his own wife, and each woman her own husband. The husband should fulfill his marital duty to his wife, and likewise the wife to her husband. The wife's body does not belong to her alone but also to her husband. In the same way, the husband's body does not belong to him alone but also to his wife. Do not deprive each other except by mutual consent and for a time, so that you may devote yourselves to prayer. Then come together again so that Satan will not tempt you because of your lack of self-control.*

The writer to the Hebrews teaches,

> *Marriage should be honored by all, and the marriage bed kept pure; for God will judge the adulterer and all the sexually immoral.*
>
> (Hebrews 13:4)

Putting covenant relationship above the issues

Marriage is a covenantal relationship of complete commitment to one another. We promise to love each other in sickness and in health until death parts us. In any close relationship there will be points of disagreement or conflict and how we handle those will determine whether it can be sustained.

We need to choose clearly to put our marriage covenant higher than issues which may arise, otherwise all the enemy will need to do is cause trouble as a result of disagreements and sooner or later one party will walk out. When difficulties come, married couples should value their relationship too much to become separated over the issues.

Covenant relationship must transcend all the issues. Understanding their individual roles will help couples in dealing with the difficulties they may face.

Summary

In summary, therefore, God's plan is for sexual intimacy to be within the context of the marriage covenant. In the next chapter we will look at the consequences of entering into sexual intimacy outside of marriage.

Notes

1. 'I Have Decided to Follow Jesus,' Broadman Press, 1959.
2. Whitaker House, 1995.
3. Prince, *The Marriage Covenant.*

Outside the Covenant

Having understood what happens in sex as God intended it to be, let us now turn our attention to what happens in ungodly sex.

Understanding soul-ties

In chapter 1 I referred to the one-flesh bonding which takes place during the act of sexual intercourse where two distinct individuals are united and become one. I said that although sex is a joining together of their two bodies, it actually involves a union of every part of them which is not just temporary. This "one-flesh" bonding means a link of spirit, soul and body. An intermingling takes place and influences from one person pass to the other. Even when there is a physical separation something intangible joins the two together.

When I am teaching this, I often ask a married couple to come forward to do a demonstration. I put a large amount of peanut butter on the husband's hand and a large amount of Marmite (or Vegemite when in Australia!) on the wife's hand, then I press their hands together to symbolize their union. When their hands are pulled apart, on each hand is both peanut butter and Marmite. Something of each has been deposited on the other.

The peanut butter represents the husband's body, soul and spirit and the Marmite represents the wife's body, soul and spirit. They now both have that which God created "them" to be as well as that which God created their spouse to be through this intermingling.

Linking or bonding in relationships is not limited to sexual intercourse. God intended that good ties should be created in all human relationships. These ties are often referred to as "soul-ties," although the areas of bonding may involve our spirit as well as our soul. We have soul-ties with parents and other members of our family. Other soul-ties are formed as a result of our own decision to develop a friendship or have contact with someone. God's plan is that all these soul-ties should be a source of blessing as we relate to each other in godly ways.

Because of sin entering the world and affecting the human race, soul-ties which God meant to be good (godly), can be bad (ungodly), or often are a mixture of both. An ungodly soul-tie is established when two people choose to do some kind of sinful activity together. A soul-tie will be ungodly when one person in a relationship sins against the other or where one person forces an act of sin upon a helpless victim. God's blessings come through godly soul-ties but Satan's curses are transferred through ungodly soul-ties.

This is why it is so vital to understand about ungodly soul-ties. It is then possible to pray effectively against curses and demonic bondages in people's lives. We can ask God to break the ungodly ties and then pray for deliverance.

What happens in ungodly sex

When a man and a woman who are not married to each other have sexual intercourse, they are consummating a "marriage" without having made a covenant of marriage. This is what I would call "unsafe sex." The world would tell us that unsafe sex is sex without a condom but that is the least of it. Unsafe sex is when we allow our spirit to be penetrated by someone else's spirit without a covenant of marriage in place.

An ungodly soul-tie is established through sexual sin. When we surrender to sexual temptation and have sex with someone to whom we are not married, an ungodly soul-tie is established and stays in place unless it is broken by God.

God is the only one who can break an ungodly soul-tie. Until it is broken, Satan has the right to use it to bring a curse upon us, because it has been established through sin. After repentance we can ask God to break the ungodly soul-ties.

I sometimes think of a soul-tie as an invisible railway line which links one person to another. These links were God's idea for our relating to one another, to strengthen one another and to be the source of mutual blessing. On the railway line, carriages of blessings would pass up and down the track. When ungodly soul-ties are established by sin, Satan hijacks the whole thing. In Romans 6:16 Paul writes:

> Don't you know ... you are slaves to the one whom you obey –
> whether you are slaves to sin, which leads to death, or to
> obedience, which leads to righteousness?

When an ungodly railway line has been established, railway carriages of cursing rather than blessings pass up and down the tracks.

Consequences of ungodly soul-ties

What sort of things can come through an ungodly soul-tie? Firstly there are physical things such as different types of sexually transmitted diseases: genital warts, herpes, gonorrhea, syphilis, HIV, hepatitis B, chlamydia and AIDS, which pass physically as an infection from one person to another in the body fluids.

Sexually transmitted diseases (STDs) are now endemic in our promiscuous western societies! Each time people have a different sexual partner, they raise their chances of contracting a sexually transmitted disease. People who have multiple sexual partners often have sex with others who are also promiscuous, thereby increasing their vulnerability to disease.

In particular, the number of cases of chlamydia is increasing rapidly and, as this disease can cause sterility in women by causing pelvic infection and damaging the Fallopian tubes, there can be serious long-term consequences. Although there are other diseases that can cause pelvic infection, chlamydia is especially significant as it often gives no symptoms during the infection, particularly in men. Therefore it can go undetected and untreated.

Since conception normally takes place in the Fallopian tubes, if they are damaged, conception cannot occur. A woman who has suffered from chlamydia may not realize there is a problem until she marries and desires to bear children. Upon failing to conceive she may go to an infertility clinic for tests. Maybe it is not until then that she will have to come to terms with the consequences of promiscuity.

Many women are concerned about not getting pregnant. They take the contraceptive pill but do not insist that their partner uses a condom, not realizing that this makes them vulnerable to contracting a sexually transmitted disease.

It is a popular misconception that, if a condom is worn, the couple is "safe" from transmitted infections. Indeed, they are certainly "safer," but condoms not infrequently split, slip off and often any plans to use them are abandoned in the passion of the moment.

In addition, there are a few diseases that only need genital contact rather than full sexual intercourse to be transmitted. These include genital warts and herpes, both of which tend to recur throughout a person's life once they have been caught. The message to all our young people today should be, "before marriage there should be absolutely no genital contact." Many who finally come for help have never been taught about these things. They have never appreciated the consequences of promiscuity.

Emotional and mental problems can come down a soul-tie too. For example, a girl who has never suffered from depression has ungodly sex with a man who suffers from depression. She can find to her horror she is now suffering from depression; she comes for help and is asked, "When did the depression begin?" "About six months ago," she says. When asked what else was happening in her life six months ago she might reply, "Well, I did get involved in a wrong relationship about that time but I have repented of that and believe I am forgiven."

Repentance and forgiveness deal with the fact of sin but do not deal with the consequences of sin. Think of it this way: another young girl, who is a Christian, goes to a disco, gets drunk and becomes involved in sexual sin, from which she finds that she is pregnant. She is horrified, and goes to her pastor, confesses and repents fully of her sin. Is she forgiven? Answer: yes. Is she still pregnant? Yes. So there is the fact of sin as one issue and the consequences as another. Ungodly soul-ties and the rights given to the enemy through them are a consequence of sexual sin.

If a person has sexual intercourse with someone who is involved in the occult (for example, a Freemason, a witch, or a New Ager) demonic power can pass down the soul-tie into them. People will explain it by saying they feel defiled in their spirits. If they are Christians, their spiritual life can become increasingly difficult. Their faith, their worship and their spiritual gifts can all become negatively affected.

By means of an ungodly soul-tie, physical disease and emotional, mental and spiritual pressure and difficulty can be transmitted in an ongoing way. Satan can use ungodly soul-ties until they are broken. If from the time he lost his virginity to the time he gets married, a man has ten sexual partners, he has become "one" with each woman. If you like he has ten wives. The fact that the relationships were over years ago still leaves the ungodly soul-ties in place, despite the fact that he has repented.

If a Christian couple have "anticipated" their marriage by entering into a premarital sexual relationship and even though they have never had intercourse with anyone else, they still need to repent of their sin and have the ungodly soul-tie broken. Before making their marriage covenant they would also need to separate sexually until after their marriage, so that the foundations of their marriage can be pure and holy.

All sin can be repented of and forgiven but we do need to do it and not try and cover it up. Sadly many couples live together as husband and wife before they are married and never deal with the consequences.

Let us ask the question, "Does it put things right for them just to get married in church?" Answer: "No!" "Can we ask God to bless a marriage which has been founded in sexual sin?" Sin gives Satan authority and we need to remove that authority. Repentance, confession, forgiveness and all ungodly soul-ties should be broken first so that the couple can enter their Christian marriage on a clear and holy foundation.

When I teach this, many couples come and tell me that their marital foundations were sinful and they have never had the ungodly soul-ties broken with all their previous sexual partners. When they sincerely repent before God and have their ungodly soul-ties cut they can feel completely new and clean on the inside.

Ungodly soul-ties within marriage through unequal yoking

The Bible does not use the word "soul-tie" but we find the concept in many places. One example is 2 Corinthians 6:14 where it says, *"Do not be yoked together with unbelievers."* I understand this to mean that when we become "yoked together" we become "soul-tied" with unbelievers. When we do this in marriage, we open up our spirits to be penetrated by all that is in the unsaved, unregenerate person in an ongoing way.

I cannot emphasize strongly enough here how foolish it is for a Christian to choose an unsaved spouse. I have many friends from my youth who did this and they are no longer in the Body of Christ today. It is a deception to think we shall "get them saved" after our marriage. If you put a good apple next to a bad apple, does the bad apple become good? Rather the good apple becomes affected by the bad. God in His mercy, of course, could save our unsaved married partner but we should never "trade" on His grace. We would be ignoring the strong warning placed in Scripture not to be unequally yoked.

What about if both parties were unsaved at the time of the marriage and one has now become saved? Paul teaches us in 1 Corinthians 7:12–17 that the believer should not leave the marriage, but if the unbeliever wants to leave, the believer is not "bound" in these circumstances. It is interesting that Paul says:

> *For the unbelieving husband has been sanctified through his wife, and the unbelieving wife has been sanctified through her believing husband. Otherwise your children would be unclean, but as it is, they are holy.*
>
> (1 Corinthians 7:14)

I believe that this means that the new Christian has more power and influence than the one who is not a Christian. Through the godly soul-tie of the believer, the unbeliever is made holy and the children of that marriage too.

> *Greater is He who is in you than he who is in the world.*
>
> (1 John 4:4 NASB)

However, flagrant rebellion against God's Word gives rights and also authority to the demonic realm. In that case there is no protection, and occult power can come down the soul-tie into the believing partner. For example, the Christian wife of a Freemason needs to protect herself spiritually by placing, in prayer, the cross of Jesus and the blood of Jesus between her and anything demonic which is trying to access her through the unbelieving partner.

We can always bind down demonic power. Jesus said,

> *"Behold, I give unto you power to tread on serpents and scorpions, and over all the power of the enemy: and nothing shall by any means hurt you."*
>
> (Luke 10:19 kjv)

We need to use the power and authority given to us by Jesus. For the believing partner in the marriage it is necessary to do warfare and to forbid any demonic power access into their spirit through sexual intercourse.

Summary

We have been looking at ungodly sex which is outside of God's original plan for human beings. Satan especially wants us to sin sexually because it interferes with our love relationship to God so that we no longer glorify and honor God in all we do. It establishes ungodly soul-ties, which Satan can use for ever unless they are broken. It causes us to submit to the enemy and gives him authority in our lives. It enables Satan to penetrate our spirits and thus defile them. As a result we may become demonized with unclean spirits.

The greatest damage as a result of sexual sin, as with all sin, is that we are separated from God. Satan rebelled in heaven and wanted to stop love, adoration and worship going to God and to have it for himself. He has never changed. In the temptations of Jesus in Luke 4:6–7 Satan says:

> *"I will give you [Jesus] all . . . authority and splendor, for it has been given to me, and I can give it to anyone I want to. So if you worship me, it will all be yours."*

Satan wants to break our relationship with God just as he did with Jesus. This helps us to understand why sexual sin is so rife.

Restoration after sexual sin and dealing with ungodly soul-ties

You may at this point be asking what hope there is for those who have already entered into the experience of sex before marriage. In 1 Corinthians 6:9–10 there is a strong warning against sexual immorality:

> *Do you not know that the wicked will not inherit the kingdom of God? Do not be deceived: Neither the sexually immoral nor idolaters nor adulterers nor male prostitutes nor homosexual offenders nor thieves nor the greedy nor drunkards nor slanderers nor swindlers will inherit the kingdom of God.*

However, the following verse continues on to say that this is what some of them were but now they have been cleansed and sanctified. This is a powerful message of encouragement and hope to all who have sinned sexually. The good news is that it is never too late to repent and Jesus will forgive and cleanse.

In addition to receiving forgiveness of sexual sin there is a need for something to be done about the joining together of body, soul and spirit which has taken place through the "one-flesh" bonding and has not been glorifying or honoring to God. There will need to be a cleansing, which is done by breaking the ungodly soul-ties and by addressing the demonic. The aim of all ministry is to see the person restored to the place they were in before they sinned, and remove Satan's rights so they can walk free. God is able!

When, following confession and repentance, we ask God to break a soul-tie we are asking Him to do three things. Firstly, we are asking Him to sever the ungodly soul-tie which connects the individual emotionally or spiritually to a previous sexual partner. Secondly, we are asking Him to remove every influence of the sexual partner from the person receiving ministry. Thirdly, we are asking God to restore to the person being prayed for everything of himself or herself that has been tied or intermingled with the other individual through this soul-tie. Following this breaking of the soul-tie, we can then take authority over all demonic spirits that have been given a right through this sin and tell them to go.

When people sincerely repent before God and have their ungodly soul-ties cut they can feel utterly new and clean on the inside. Many have written to me to say that, having dealt with ungodly soul-ties, their marriage has taken on a completely new dimension. They feel totally disconnected from their past and able to relate together in a deeper, fresher way.

Let us return now to the first girl I mentioned, who was depressed after sexual sin but had fully repented. We will need to ask Jesus to break the ungodly soul-tie that has been established between her and the man she sinned sexually with. We would do this using a prayer along the following lines:

> *In the name of the Father, Son and Holy Spirit, I speak out a breaking of the ungodly tie existing between _____ and _____* (name the individuals). *I ask You, Lord, to sever that linking in the spiritual realms and to separate completely and bring total cleansing between every part of _____ and every part of _____. I ask this in Jesus' name. Amen.*

After hearing this teaching and receiving ministry along these lines one person wrote:

> The teaching has given me a deep understanding about God's original, perfect and marvelous creation and His way to live a life in dignity within a fallen and distorted world. He has given me back the parts of myself which I left in premarital sexual relationships before I was born again. He has forgiven me my sins in my thoughts and in my soul and set me free from my bondage to them.

If you have sinned in the sexual area God is able to do the same for you.

The Struggle with Sexual Sin

4

We have looked at what happens in godly and ungodly sex. In this chapter we shall explore some of the reasons why so many people struggle with sexual sin issues.

Understanding our carnal nature

First and foremost we struggle with sexual sin issues in our lives because we have a carnal nature. It is that self-centered part of our being that wants what we think is best for us rather than what God thinks is best for us. It is that part of our being that wants to operate outside of God's plans for our life and well-being and is in rebellion to God.

As a result of the Fall, we have all inherited a carnal or sinful nature. By choosing to rebel against God and disobey His commands, Adam and Eve submitted to the desires of the flesh and came into the knowledge of evil. They discovered that short-term pleasure can have long-term consequences. The apostle James warns us,

> but each one is tempted when, by his own evil desire, he is dragged away and enticed. Then, after desire has conceived, it gives birth to sin; and sin, when it is full-grown, gives birth to death. Don't be deceived, my dear brothers.
>
> (James 1:14–16)

When we become Christians our carnal nature does not simply vanish. Yes – our eternal destiny in Jesus changes. Yes – through the Holy Spirit we have a new source of strength to call upon, but no – we don't miraculously find we are no longer troubled by sin issues. Even though we are saved we still find we are in a battle with temptation. We still struggle with *"the cravings of sinful man, the lust of his eyes"* (1 John 2:16).

We are told by Paul that we must put away our carnal nature and instead be led by the Spirit. He recognizes that we are in a battle and instructs us to make right choices in the way we express our sexuality. For some, making those right choices will be even harder where there has been emotional deprivation or where the consequences of sexual sin on the generational line have created a weakness for sin in the area of their sexuality.

Understanding the emotional root causes of sexual sin

Some people can feel rootless, hungry for touch and relationship, with no sense of being. Perhaps they never knew their mother's tender touch or their father's affirmation and embrace. They feel terribly afraid and yet are not able to understand or define it. Often the sufferer cannot put into words what they are afraid of. This could be because something happened to them at a time of life which pre-dated their language. Early damage in their childhood is echoing into their life as an adult. As a result they are unnaturally fearful.

They cannot put into words the agony of not having connected with mother love. They experience stress in their adult life and may, as a result, have a sexually promiscuous lifestyle – trying to connect with someone. There is a direct link between separation anxiety and sexual sin as they try to deal with the pain their way. The One who loves them most wants them to connect to Him. He wants them to yield to Him and trust Him as their loving heavenly Father.

Healing for them is not just about "kicking out the demons," although it is true that demons feed on pain, hurts and wounds. In healing, the message of the cross has to reach all the unhealed areas. Only the cross of Jesus is able to bring the remedy for our sin, our carnal nature and the way we have tried to take control ourselves without God. On the cross God, the Creator, identifies Himself with the suffering of His created beings and takes the punishment of sin upon Himself.

I like to say, when I am teaching, that our emotional needs for love can be pictured as a tank which needs filling with love. Some people unfortunately have an empty tank. Let's suppose that a man and a woman meet and they both have empty "love tanks." I shall call them "Mr Empty Love Tank" and "Miss Empty Love Tank." Each one is hoping for personal happiness in relationship, but neither has anything to give the other. Each one is hoping the other will provide for their deep unmet needs, which reach right back into their childhood.

What they fail to understand is that true love delights in giving rather than taking from the other person. They may also have confused sex with love and become involved in sexual activity. After entering into relationships of any kind they may experience deep disillusionment and disappointment because their expectations are not being met.

The consequences of generational sin

Whilst we all may experience temptation, the nature and degree of that temptation is affected by what our ancestors have done. Their actions and decisions mean that following generations have a weakness, or propensity, to certain sins and demons are able to gain rights in the family line. Of course the tendency to sin also comes down everybody's generational line right from the Fall of man described in Genesis chapter 3.

We have seen how God's plan is to bring blessing through the human family. Deuteronomy 7:9 says:

Know therefore that the LORD your God is God; he is the faithful
God keeping his covenant of love to a thousand generations of
those who love him and keep his commands.

God's plan is to bless a thousand generations, but sin and
disobedience can rob the generations of this blessing and allow
a curse to fall on families. Mercifully the curse is limited to three
or four generations.

"I, the LORD your God, am a jealous God, visiting the iniquity
of the fathers upon the children to the third and fourth
generation of those who hate Me."

(Exodus 20:5 NKJV)

When looking at our ancestors in our family tree, the question
to ask is: "What sort of people were they?" Many of us would
think that we don't know anything about our previous family
members, but we know this: they were all sinners.

for all have sinned and fall short of the glory of God . . .

(Romans 3:23)

Exactly what type of sins did they commit? It is these sins which
will be repeated in our family line. Parents are entrusted by God
with the spiritual covering of their children until the age of
individuation. That covering can be pictured as a spiritual
umbrella that the parents are holding over their children. If the
umbrella has a hole in it, where would the children get wet?
Answer: in the area under the hole.

If one or both parents were in some sort of sexual sin, then
the children may be "covered" or protected in every other area,
but there is a defective covering or hole in the area of sexual sin.
We could, therefore, expect that the children could themselves
have a built-in weakness for sexual sin.

It is well understood that children can inherit a physical
weakness such as heart disease. In a similar fashion children can

inherit the propensity to sexual sin, being strongly tempted by
the enemy. Thus they repeat the sins of their fathers and pass
down this inherited spiritual weakness to their own children.

However, it will still be a free-will choice for each person in
the family to commit sin or to resist it. We do not have to
repeat the sin of our family line, because 1 Corinthians 10:13
says:

> *No temptation has seized you except what is common to man.
> And God is faithful; he will not let you be tempted beyond what
> you can bear. But when you are tempted, he will also provide a
> way out so that you can stand up under it.*

David and Bathsheba

Let's take a look at the story of David and Bathsheba in 2 Samuel
11. *"In the spring, at the time when kings go off to war . . . David
remained in Jerusalem."* He was where he should not have been
and he was idle. He should, as king, have been leading his men
into the battle. Frequently sexual sin can happen when we are
not where we should be. From the roof of his palace he saw a
beautiful woman taking a bath. What was she doing naked in
view of the palace roof? Maybe she was not behaving as a
married woman should. David saw her. He could not help the
first look but then he should have looked away and turned his
attention to something else – but that was not what happened.

David was a man after God's own heart, the anointed king.
He knew right from wrong but he allowed temptation to grow
in his mind. All temptations start in the mind. The battleground
for our purity and holiness is there. (In 2 Corinthians 10:5 we are
told to *"take captive every thought to make it obedient to Christ."*)
David asked his aides, "Who is that woman?" He may not have
known who Bathsheba was, but when he was told it was Uriah's
wife he certainly knew who Uriah the Hittite was.

In 1 Chronicles 11 there is a list of the men of valor who
protected David's back when he was fleeing from Saul. Uriah

the Hittite is among them (v. 41). This was not just anybody's wife but the wife of a faithful friend who had risked his own life probably on more than one occasion to save David's neck. David already had many wives and he knew the Ten Commandments: *"You shall not commit adultery."*

We might have expected better from the king but he sent for her, having already decided what he was going to do (2 Samuel 11:4). He could have turned back and even when she arrived at the palace, he could have said "no" to sin and "yes" to God. He slept with her, probably only ever expecting this to be a "one-night stand." Verse 4 tells us she had purified herself from her uncleanness. What does this mean? She had just finished a period. This is important information because it tells us that the child that was conceived could not have possibly been Uriah's child. She had already had a period after her husband had left her for the war, so she was not pregnant by him. This was definitely David's child.

Trying to hide the truth

> *The woman conceived and sent word to David, saying, "I am pregnant."*
>
> (2 Samuel 11:5)

The world would say, "Bad luck, David, after only one night with her." So David proceeded with Plan A – which was to summon Uriah back from the war and get him to sleep with his wife. David's sin could then remain a secret and Uriah could be said to be the father of the baby. Plan A failed because fighting men agreed together while a war was on to put all their energy into fighting. Winning the war was the very best way to serve the king and protect their wives and families. Uriah was a man of his word and he did not sleep with his wife.

Now for Plan B, which was to get Uriah drunk. Alcohol can be something which removes our normal inhibitions and can turn people on sexually. David thought if he got Uriah really drunk, he would go to his wife and have sex with her and David would have covered his sin, but Plan B failed too.

This meant David getting into deeper sin as he moved to Plan C. David wrote to Joab, his commander in the war, and told him to put Uriah in the heat of the battle and withdraw from him. What had Uriah done to deserve death at the hand of the king, whom he undoubtedly loved and served whole-heartedly? David gave Uriah his own death warrant to take to Joab when he returned to the battle. David had now sunk into murder and deception, as well as adultery.

Finally Bathsheba was told, "Uriah is dead!" After she had mourned for him the requisite number of days, David took her into his palace. This was a terrible deception as the common people (in a day before widows' pensions) would have thought, "Haven't we got a truly wonderful king. He has taken this war widow into his own home to provide for her!"

Tracing David's sin back to the beginning, it all began with one night of passion with a beautiful woman, but of course that was Satan's strategy for the anointed King of Israel. Satan wanted David up to his neck in sin and disobedience to the Word of God. He committed adultery, he lied, he deceived, he used his power as king to get the true husband murdered and finally he did a "cover-up job" – *"But the thing David had done displeased the LORD"* (2 Samuel 11:27).

Confronted by the truth

I heard of a pastor who committed adultery and had a three-year affair with a married woman in his church. Many people confronted him with his "wrong relationship" but he repeatedly denied it. Like David, God gave him "a window of opportunity to repent," but unlike David he did not – and then God exposed the sin for all to see. God in His grace will always give people an opportunity to repent. I do not know how long the window remains open but the time comes when it is shut and God will then expose the sin.

Nathan arrived at the palace and told David (the ex-shepherd boy) the story of the poor man who had a pet lamb. It ate from his plate and drank from his cup. A rich man was expecting visitors and they rather fancied lamb stew for the menu that night. The rich man, who had many lambs himself, took the poor man's pet lamb and killed it and gave it to his visitors.

David was indignant. His sin was by now so deeply covered up that perhaps it no longer troubled his conscience. Nathan eventually confronts him directly, *"You are the man!"* (2 Samuel 12:7). David finally came in deep heart-broken repentance towards God and in Psalm 51 there is not a single hint of justification for his sin:

> *Against You, You only, have I sinned,*
> *And done this evil in Your sight...*
>
> (v. 4 NKJV)

What I find totally amazing is not just that God forgave David, but that He allowed him to have Bathsheba as his wife. God even allowed Jesus to be born into the resulting family line, descended from this marriage. Although the baby conceived out of wedlock died, Bathsheba had another son, Solomon, who succeeded David as king.

God's restoring heart

Both of the genealogies relating to Jesus found in the New Testament trace His line back to David and Bathsheba. Matthew's genealogy concerning Joseph, who was the foster father of Jesus, even records that *"David was the father of Solomon, whose mother had been Uriah's wife"* (Matthew 1:6b). It was this genealogy that determined that Joseph had to go to Bethlehem (which was his home town) for the census and why Jesus was born in Bethlehem – the city of David and not Nazareth. Joseph, of course, had nothing biologically to do with

Jesus who was born of a virgin – *"because what is conceived in her*
[Mary] *is from the Holy Spirit"* (Matthew 1:20).

Very interestingly, the genealogy in Luke's Gospel (Luke
3:23–37), which most commentators consider to be the ancestry
of Mary, traces back to another Nathan, whom we read in
1 Chronicles 3:5 was the son of David and Bathsheba. So both
Mary and Joseph were born of David's line and descended from
the marriage of David and Bathsheba.

This gives us an incredible insight into the restoring heart of
God, not only to forgive, but also to restore again after failure,
appalling sexual sin, deception and murder. David had broken
at least three of the Ten Commandments: "You shall not
murder," "You shall not commit adultery" and "You shall
not covet your neighbor's wife." Although David had other
wives whom God could have used to send His only begotten
Son into the world He chose to do so through the offspring of
the marriage of David and Bathsheba.

This encourages me to know that sexual sin and even murder
are not unforgivable sins and, for the truly repentant, there is
not only forgiveness but complete restoration after failure. God
restores us just as if we had never sinned.

God forgave David. God did not tell David he was no longer
fit to be the anointed king. Neither did He instruct David and
Bathsheba to separate for the rest of their lives, which maybe is
how many church leaders would deal with a similar situation
today. Despite David's failure God chose to send His Son into the
world through David's line and be born in David's hometown.

There is a cycle of sin which goes like this:

- I saw
- I coveted
- I took, or stole it
- I hid.

This is what Adam and Eve did in the Garden of Eden. This
is what Achan did with the devoted things (Joshua 6–7). This is

what David did here. We too need to beware of this cycle of sin in our own lives.

Sin on David's generational line

I want to illustrate something else from this account of David's life. Sexual sin was clearly on his generational line. Ten generations before David we get that rather strange story of Tamar. She was widowed and, feeling that she had been wrongly treated by her dead husband's family, finally dressed herself up as a prostitute and enticed her father-in-law (Judah) to have sex with her. The result was that she had twin boys, Perez and Zerah (Genesis 38:29–30). These twins were certainly born of a forbidden marriage.

In Deuteronomy 23:2 it says,

> No one born of a forbidden marriage [illegitimately] nor any of his descendants may enter the assembly of the LORD, even down to the tenth generation.

Illegitimacy is one of those very strong inherited weaknesses that can come down the generational line. David also had an illegitimate child who died. In fact some Bible commentators think that when David says in Psalm 51, *"in sin my mother conceived me"* (NKJV), he is referring to his own illegitimacy.

It is interesting that when the prophet Samuel comes to anoint one of the sons of Jesse as the future king, Jesse assembles his sons for Samuel's inspection. At the end of the line Samuel says in effect, "It's none of these – do you have any more?" Only after this does Jesse say he has a young lad looking after the sheep. If David is referring to his own illegitimacy in Psalm 51, it would explain why his father Jesse did not include him with his other sons. Perhaps he was born as a result of a sexual relationship outside of marriage.

David's sons went on into dreadful sexual sin. In 2 Samuel 13 there is the story of David's son Amnon raping his half-sister

Tamar. Absalom, another of David's sons, finally murders Amnon for this act. Here we can see the acts of sexual sin and murder by David, passing down to his sons, who repeated David's sins in their own lives.

Many of us may have sexual sin on our family line. It is not our fault. (We didn't choose our parents and grandparents.) We may, however, have a hole in our spiritual covering in the area of sexual sin.

Broken marriages and illegitimacy may be the consequences of the sins of our ancestors. We may have been uncovered in these areas and therefore we became vulnerable to repeating the same sins in our lives. This does not mean that we can blame our parents for the fact that we have repeated their sins in our own lives. We still have a will and can make godly choices but whatever is on our family line gives us a "push" or a pre-disposition to sin in the same way as they did.

Dealing with the sins of the ancestors

When Jesus said on the cross, *"It is finished!"* (John 19:30), He had not only died for our sins, but also for the sins of our fathers. We need firstly to confess (that means agree with God), that our forbears were sinners, forgive them and ask Jesus to cut us off from the visiting of their iniquity upon us through His death on the cross. In Ellel Ministries we thoroughly pray into a person's family tree and cut them off from all their known inherited weaknesses (body, soul and spirit) in the name of Jesus.

During ministry we invite people to say a prayer along the following lines:

> *I unreservedly forgive all my ancestors for all the things that they have done which have affected me and my life. I confess* [agree with God's verdict upon] *and renounce* [personally turn away from] *all of their sinful activities, specifically* _____ (speak out known sins including occult activity and sexual sin). *I claim my freedom*

from the consequences of these sins, from all generational curses and pronouncements, and from all hereditary diseases. Thank You, Jesus, that You became cursed for me and that Your blood was shed so that I might be set free. Amen.

Each Christian should do this. Then of course, as we are holding the spiritual umbrella over our own children, and the hole is dealt with, it will no longer affect succeeding generations. (If our children are at a place where they can make their own decisions, or over the age of eighteen, they will need to do this for themselves.)

This is applying the finished work of Calvary to our lives because it does not happen automatically at salvation! Jesus said,

"In My name they will cast out demons . . . they will lay hands on the sick, and they will recover."

(Mark 16:17, 18 NKJV)

We would not need to go and do it, if it was fully dealt with the moment each person became a believer. As Christians we need to apply the finished work of the cross individually into our own lives. It is all dealt with at the cross but we then have to apply the various aspects of the cross. Philippians 2:12 says, *"work out your own salvation with fear and trembling."* Jesus has done it all; now we have to receive it all.

In the next chapter we will look at some of the ways in which people submit to temptation and are enticed into sexual activity which is outside of God's plans for His creation and therefore sinful.

Sleeping with the Enemy

5

Having considered why so many people struggle with sexual sin issues, let us look in some detail at what sexual sin is, so that we can begin to understand the various ways in which the enemy tries to ensnare people in his trap and gain footholds in their lives.

Premarital sex or fornication (including trial marriages)

Until recently in the English-speaking world couples who lived together and were not married were said to be living "in sin." However, the phrase has now become unfashionable and nobody is ever heard using it. But what about other cultures and societies? While on a visit to Ghana, in Africa, I was shocked to be told that no African would consider marrying a wife he had not "road-tested" first!

Despite these so-called cultural norms, the Bible is quite clear that sexual intercourse is only for and within the covenant of marriage and all sexual relationships before marriage are outside of God's plans and purposes. This is sin, and will give the enemy authority and rights in the lives of those who enter into such relationships. God's Word transcends the cultural setting that we live in and never changes.

The New Testament was written in Greek and the earliest versions of the English Bible translated the word *porneia* as "fornication." This refers to sexual intercourse between individuals who are not married. More modern versions of the Bible translate this word as "immorality." There are a number of Bible passages, such as those quoted below, which clearly teach us to avoid fornication or immorality.

> *Flee from sexual immorality. All other sins a man commits are outside his body, but he who sins sexually sins against his own body. Do you not know that your body is a temple of the Holy Spirit, who is in you, whom you have received from God? You are not your own; you were bought at a price. Therefore honor God with your body.*
>
> (1 Corinthians 6:18–20)

> *For this you know, that no fornicator, unclean person, nor covetous man, who is an idolater, has any inheritance in the kingdom of Christ and God.*
>
> (Ephesians 5:5 NKJV)

> *It is God's will that you should be sanctified: that you should avoid sexual immorality.*
>
> (1 Thessalonians 4:3)

Pre-marriage counseling is extremely important for believers. Courtship should center on the spirit and the soul, not around the body. If a couple promise God and each other to keep themselves pure and only for each other until after the covenant of marriage has been made, then clear boundaries need to be in place to enable that to happen. The engaged couple should be in a place of accountability to their leaders or elders and should agree together what is appropriate behavior for them before the wedding and stick to it.

Such things as heavy petting are intended to be foreplay to intercourse and to enter into these with the intention of stopping short of intercourse can be foolhardy at worst and frustrating at best.

If a couple is determined not to enter into pre-marital sex, then all their behavior needs to reinforce that decision. One thing can quickly lead to another and sexual sin can take place. Maybe this was never intended by the two parties, but it was Satan's plan for them. It is extremely difficult to put the clock back on sexual behavior which was intended to be progressive within marriage. It is very difficult to stop and walk away once touching of one another's sexual parts has begun. Therefore courtship should not be centered on the body, but on getting to know each other's personalities and relating well emotionally. It is a great time for enjoying doing fun things together and sharing a sense of humor.

I believe that today, dating one to one starts far too early. Young people, instead of hanging out together in groups, begin dating at an increasingly early age. At the same time, with university education becoming the norm and the cost of housing escalating, the age for marriage is becoming later. The average age of people entering into marriage for the first time in the UK in 2000 was thirty-five years for men and thirty-two for women according to government released statistics.

If a girl from the age of twelve is allowed to date one to one, go to the cinema or to a disco with a boy of fourteen, will she still be pure by the age of twenty-six when she gets married? I wonder if she is really just going to kiss for the next fourteen years. Christian parents and leaders need to be aware of the statistics. Many Christian young people have had sexual experience before marriage and some have even contracted sexually transmitted diseases. Although it is extremely difficult to put into practice in the social climate of today, it might be better for believers not to have one-to-one dating until they reach the age of eighteen and then they should carefully consider what boundaries they are going to stay within.

I believe that the idea of staying out all night at parties in mixed groups or single people going on holiday alone together or sharing accommodation without an adult present, to whom they are accountable, should also be avoided. If a Christian is serious about being obedient to God, who requires chastity before marriage and fidelity afterwards, his or her lifestyle needs to reflect this. Marriage is not just about sex. Marriage is about the mutual sharing of our lives, which are laid down for each other, and is for the rest of our lives together. The courtship phase of a relationship before the wedding should be a time when the couple are getting to know each other and are establishing a firm foundation of friendship upon which to build their lives together. If they become sexually active, this activity quickly becomes the focus of their relationship.

Adultery

In normal everyday speech the word "adultery" means sexual intercourse between a married person and someone who is not his or her legal partner. In the Bible and particularly in the Old Testament the word is used in a much wider context to mean any kind of sexual immorality, for example *"You shall not commit adultery"* (Exodus 20:14).

We have looked at length at the sin of adultery between David and Bathsheba and how the enemy had a major strategy for David's life to bring him out of the purposes of God. This is an example of two married people having sexual intercourse outside of their marriage covenants, but in the New Testament Jesus extends the meaning of the sin of adultery to include adultery in the heart:

> *"You have heard that it was said, 'Do not commit adultery.' But I tell you that anyone who looks at a woman lustfully has already committed adultery with her in his heart."*
> (Matthew 5:27–28)

If a person looks at someone else and fantasizes about having sex with them, Jesus says, although no bodily contact has taken place, the sin of adultery has happened in the person's mind, emotions and will. We will return to this again when considering the matter of pornography.

Incest

The sin of sexual intercourse between people who are so closely related that marriage is prohibited is usually referred to as incest. Although the word "incest" does not appear in the Bible we read,

> *"None of you shall approach anyone who is near of kin to him, to uncover his nakedness: I am the LORD."*
>
> (Leviticus 18:6 NKJV)

Leviticus 18:6–18 explains in detail what "near of kin" means and it is interesting that the instructions about forbidden sexual relationships are addressed to men.

God has given each one of us boundaries and a man should not be sexually attracted to female close family members. It causes families to break down and that is why God's Word gives us safe boundaries. Even the unsaved know this is wrong, a point Paul himself makes when dealing with the issue of incest,

> *It is actually reported that there is sexual immorality among you, and of a kind that does not occur even among pagans: A man has his father's wife.*
>
> (1 Corinthians 5:1)

Freedom from condemnation

We minister into many people's lives who have broken God's commands and have committed sexual sin. When they truly turn, repent and say, "I never want that sin to be in my life again. I hate it as God does. I choose with God's help to put my feet on a holy path, and be the pure, blameless, holy servant of God He has called me to be," we then see that God comes to begin a process of cleansing, healing and restoration.

It is His grace, mercy and unconditional love to want to forgive and redeem sinners. He does call for deep repentance which must be walked in for the rest of our life. Jesus said to the woman caught in adultery, *"Neither do I condemn you; go and sin no more"* (John 8:11 NKJV).

Some Christians feel that they have badly "blown it." They imagine God will say, "Go and sit on the back row and just keep your head down." If this is you, the good news is that God wants not only to bring healing and restoration to a broken life, but He wants to use it for His glory.

Distorted by the Enemy

We have looked at how Satan tries to ensnare people in his trap and gain footholds in their lives, but he also perverts or distorts the natural sexual instincts so that they deviate from any normal expression of our God-given sexuality. We have seen how God's perfect plan is that the expression of our sexuality should be in a loving marriage relationship.

I believe our sexuality is distorted when it is expressed in a non-loving environment or in a way that is inconsistent with the anatomy God created for men and women. Sexuality expressed in such ways devalues one of God's beautiful gifts and leads to demonic bondage.

It is necessary in this chapter to look at some of the ways the expression of sexuality has become distorted, not because it is in any way edifying but because *"my people are destroyed from lack of knowledge"* (Hosea 4:6). We need to be aware of the enemy's schemes if we are to set people free from demonic bondages and bring healing into their lives. Jesus gave His disciples *"authority to trample on snakes and scorpions and to overcome all the power of the enemy"* (Luke 10:19).

Anal sex

God never intended the anus or back passage to be penetrated for sex. All the sphincter muscles go downwards to facilitate the evacuation of the bowel. Anal sex therefore is usually painful and blood can be shed. It occurs to me that this could be Satan's counterfeit of the shedding of blood as a marriage covenant is being consummated.

People, both men and women, who have been victims in their past to anal handling and anal abuse, can go on to want anal sex in their marriage. In all probability the ungodly soul-tie with the abuser has never been broken and demonization will have taken place. There is usually a spirit driving this, which needs to be addressed.

People who have had anal sex can later suffer with such problems as irritable bowel syndrome, infections and abnormalities of the lower bowel. Nightly anal itching can have a spiritual root and the ungodly soul-tie with the anal abuser may need to be broken and the spirit of infirmity addressed.

If a Christian husband is asking his wife for anal sex he should stop it and seek help from someone who understands how to minister into the roots, which will be in his own abusive past or on his generational line. Wives do not have to submit to this. God never requires us to submit to a demon or to perverted sexual behavior.

Oral sex

There is no clear scripture which says, "Thou shalt not have oral sex"; however, anatomically it is very obvious that God has provided the vagina as the correct body opening or orifice for a wife to receive her husband's penis.

To be explicit about oral sex, I am not talking here about a wife kissing or touching her husband's genitalia in foreplay prior to intercourse. I am talking about full ejaculation into the mouth or throat. I believe such oral sex to be a perversion – that is, a simulation of the sex act but using the mouth instead of the vagina.

Homosexual men do not have a vagina and therefore will have oral or anal sex together. I do not believe that oral sex is a godly practice even within a Christian marriage – it can replace healthy normal sexual interaction and often "oral sex" needs supersede the normal and displace the vaginal sexual relationship.

Experientially we find that women who have had oral sex (and usually to please their husband not themselves) can suffer from such things as streptococcal infections of the throat and mouth and ulcers that do not respond to treatment. Sometimes when women receive prayer, deliverance is necessary because they have been affected spiritually as well as physically. If these women do not seem to be able to move in the spiritual gifts, such as tongues, it is often because an "unholy" spirit is sitting on their mouth acting as a barrier. When they repent of oral sex, and maybe forgive the man too, deliverance from this spirit often means they are then released into speaking in tongues and the exercise of other gifts.

Let us consider how many of the gifts of the Holy Spirit use the mouth: speaking in tongues, interpretation of tongues, prophecy, words of knowledge, words of wisdom, not to mention the gifts of teaching the Word of God and preaching the gospel. Maybe we should understand better than we do how important it is to God that our mouths are holy and are instruments of righteousness.

We should include here that much filthy language and swearing is sexually rooted and believers need to take note of James chapter 3 where we read,

> *The tongue also is a fire, a world of evil among the parts of the body. It corrupts the whole person, sets the whole course of his life on fire, and is itself set on fire by hell ... Out of the same mouth come praise and cursing. My brothers this should not be. Can both fresh water and salt water flow from the same spring?*
> (vv. 6, 10–11)

We should have a clean mouth, certainly clear of all blasphemy and all sexual or other swear words. We need to seek the

Lord in deep repentance and ask for His cleansing, that He alone will use our mouths and no other spirit will control them.

Sexual bondage games

The enemy's ultimate purpose for mankind is spiritual and physical death. We should not forget this when we consider sexual bondage games. This is where a person has to be tied up, usually with strong rubber webbing or similar material, which disables them. Sexual arousal then takes place, stopping at the key psychological moment. Often the bound person is asked to beg or do something else very humiliating in order for the unbound person to continue the sex game or "tease."

A number of years ago there was considerable media coverage and interest when Michael Hutchence, rock star and boyfriend of television presenter Paula Yates, was found dead in a hotel room supposedly following an "auto erotic asphyxiation" bondage game that "went wrong." Paula herself died of a drugs overdose shortly afterwards. I believe that inside or outside of marriage all forms of bondage are perversion and wrong. What may seem to be a "game" may have a more sinister plan from the enemy. A Christian should never get involved in bondage or sex games.

Masochism

A masochist is a person who gets pleasure from suffering pain and gets sexually aroused by having pain inflicted. They can no longer have an orgasm unless someone is beating or hurting them. There is a need for painful interaction that has no heart in it. This person has no capacity to "feel." Their body has not been awakened by proper loving touch. This practice is an obvious distortion of God's plan which is for the expression of sexual intimacy within the security of a loving marriage relationship.

Sadism

Sadism is when one person enjoys being cruel to another – sadistic sex is even more dangerous than masochistic sex because the demons can "take over" or control a person so that he or she will only enjoy sex when someone else is screaming out in pain. Maybe they hate women because of their own dysfunctional home life and the awakening of the sex drive drives them to want to inflict pain on women.

Sadism in child abuse, for example, involves unspeakable emotional pain as well as physical pain and willful cruelty. We see evidence of that in cases where babies have been physically abused, neglected and maltreated, suffering broken bones and bruises and even having cigarettes stubbed out on them. Many have died at the hand of sadists. In Satanic worship child sacrifice is the ultimate goal. The desire of the perpetrators to make the death as slow and tortuous as possible with sexual over- or undertones simply has to be demonically driven. Satan requires child sacrifice, with death often preceded by a cruelly tortured life.

Misogyny – hatred of women

Hatred of women by a man can be the result of complete domination and control by his mother. One might say there is a "sick" umbilical cord connecting him with his mother, causing her to live her life through him. Maybe the father left and he is all she has, and so she hangs on to him. A mother can make her son to be her male emotional companion. This can also happen between mother and daughter. It leads to a very sick feeling of being invaded or violated. In ministry, the ungodly soul-tie with the mother, which still swallows or engulfs in an ungodly way, will need to be thoroughly dealt with.

Fetishes

A fetish is a particular object, practice, part of a body, or behavior, which arouses a person sexually. The fetish can become the only thing that the person relates to sexually. It can include such things as a fixation with items of clothing made of leather, denim, plastic, rubber or silk.

The use of fetishes takes the focus away from a relationship with a person and is therefore outside God's plan for sexual expression. Those who need fetishes to turn them on sexually have generally experienced some form of emotional deprivation in childhood.

Summary

In this chapter we have been looking at some of the ways in which the expression of sexuality can be distorted by the enemy even within the marriage relationship. In the next chapter we will look at how sexual expression in the absence of any partner, and totally outside of any loving covenantal relationship of marriage, can damage sexuality and result in demonic bondage.

Alone with the Enemy

God's plan was for the expression of our sexuality to be in a loving marriage relationship. The expression of our sexuality alone, in isolation from any other human being, is a trap of the enemy. His whole purpose is to lure men and women away from God's will and cause them to do *his* will which is always the very opposite to God's. Self-centered sexual arousal and release is an activity leading to deep bondage. In the extreme it can become the doorway or driving force for such abhorrent activities as rape or child abuse. In this chapter we will look at how this trap of the enemy is being laid.

Pornography

With the increasing accessibility to the Internet, the sin of pornography has escalated. The greatest use of the Internet, far exceeding all other combined use for education, travel or shopping, is for pornography. In the same way that junk mail is received through the post, so junk "spam" (containing unsolicited pornography) can be received when using the Internet or mobile phones.

Pornography can be a problem for Christians as well as non-Christians. Over a million men went to stadiums for the "Promise Keepers" Christian men's conferences in 1997. In research conducted by Promise Keepers 62 per cent of men interviewed admitted struggling with all kinds of sexual sin – including pornography.

While there is no Bible verse which says, "Thou shalt not watch pornography," we find the psalmist saying, *"I will set before my eyes no vile thing"* (Psalm 101:3b), Jesus saying, *"If your right eye causes you to sin, gouge it out and throw it away"* (Matthew 5:29), the apostle Paul teaching, *"whatsoever things are pure, whatsoever things are lovely . . . think on these things"* (Philippians 4:8 KJV), and the apostle John saying, *"For everything in the world – the cravings of sinful man, the lust of his eyes and the boasting of what he has and does – comes not from the Father but from the world"* (1 John 2:16).

Someone has foolishly called pornography the victimless crime. Women married to pornography addicts would not agree; neither would the children abused by them.

> *Death and Destruction are never satisfied,*
> *and neither are the eyes of man.*
> (Proverbs 27:20)

Men usually start by watching erotica and soft porn, which are basically nude women in seductive stances. They may progress to soft porn videos, often showing explicit sex scenes. Their viewing may then gravitate to group sex, lesbian and homosexual sex, masochistic and sadistic sex, bondage sex, and bestiality.

Pornographic material involving children (pedophile sex), sexual abuse and satanic sexual abuse (which can end with human sacrifice on film – known as "snuff videos") is illegal in the UK, the USA and many other countries. Those caught providing or watching it can be prosecuted.

Because men have a visual sexual response, the Internet is, I believe, one of Satan's most successful tools against Christian men. A Christian man has to be very careful about his eyes; "lust of the eyes" is obviously what Jesus is referring to in

Matthew 5:27–28: *"anyone who looks at a woman lustfully has already committed adultery with her in his heart."*

Men and women are "wired up" differently physically and sexually, and are aroused sexually in different ways. Men have a visual sexual response and drive – that is, they are "turned on" by what they see. This is why such sins as pornography tend to be mostly, but not exclusively, male sins.

Men no longer have to go to the porn shop, the sex shop or have materials sent under plain cover from Amsterdam. They simply have to switch on their computer and in three clicks or less they can access pornography sites. There it is accessible and available wherever they are in the world twenty-four hours per day. As men embark on it out of curiosity or "just for a laugh" to start with, the enemy has a powerful strategy against them.

The deception of pornography

It can seem so innocuous to begin with: those who watch pornography are not hurting anyone and they feel they can turn it off as soon as they want to, but this is not true. For the male, sexual desire is physically based. The desire for sexual intercourse is stimulated by the build-up of sperm cells and seminal fluid in the seminal vesicles. When the seminal vesicles are full there is a physical push for release. This physical push is driven by what is visually seen, therefore pornography promotes the whole cycle, which normally culminates in masturbatory and fantasy sex as its immediate expression.

The pornography victim fantasizes that he is having sex with the images he sees, or he copies what the players in the video are doing, as he masturbates. All sex involves using the human spirit and so what he is actually doing is joining his own spirit to the spirit behind the pornography and opening himself up to demonization.

Pornography is hugely addictive, and is also very defiling spiritually. The desire to watch with greater frequency, for longer periods and go into worse and worse sites, is driven onwards by the demonic. It quickly goes from a demonic foothold to a demonic stronghold and then to a bondage. After a short period of time of using pornography a man is in satanic chains and is a captive to the demons which now control him. Spirits of pornography, masturbation, fantasy, lust, unclean spirits and defiling spirits pollute his body, soul and spirit. He is caught in Satan's web of sexual sin. Pornography can start to disintegrate a healthy sense of being because there is an element in it that is anti-relational and impersonal.

After a while he is controlled by pornography, whether or not he watches the images, because he discovers he cannot switch them "off" from his mind. It is like a great channel of filth that has been dug across his mind, his thinking and his imagination. The pictures, the words and the images are on the front screen of his mind and constantly replay. He would like to be free of it all now but does not know how to reverse what he once made a will choice to do, feeling simply powerless to stop. Pornography is idolatry and it is illusory – of nothing that really exists. Because the evil is so illusory in the pornography it can undermine a sense of personhood. This is very destructive.

Controlled by pornography

Phillip (not his real name) came to me following one of my teaching seminars on godly sex and sexuality. He was an elder in his church and was very ashamed to confess his problem of pornography. His wife had always told him that he was "over-sexed" and as a Christian he did not want to get involved in affairs, so he had slipped into pornography very easily, getting up in the night, telling his wife it was insomnia and surfing the Net, progressing into deeper and deeper sites. He masturbated and fantasized and for a short time only it was pleasurable – then it quickly became compulsive. Whenever he did make love to his wife, he was fantasizing she was one of the girls he had seen in the pornography.

Soon he could not enjoy "straight sex" and he found he was only using his wife's body to copy pornographic sexual acts he had seen. His wife sensed in her spirit something was dreadfully wrong and soon found out what it was. This led to terrible rows, and she moved into the spare bedroom refusing him any sexual intimacy. She said she felt "groped" not loved which of course was exactly what was happening. Her rejection of him eventually caused him to reject himself, feeling guilty and ashamed. He withdrew from fellowship with other Christians and isolated himself yet further.

He told me "all joy" had gone out of his life. God seemed distant. He no longer enjoyed anything, not his faith in Jesus, his church role, his wife and his marriage or his job. In the office he had found it increasingly difficult to concentrate and his job performance had noticeably dropped. His work colleagues became aware of a decline in his motivation. He no longer cracked jokes or whistled in the corridors. He didn't want anyone with whom he had previously been friendly to come close in case they found out about his secret life. This secret life seemed like another life all of its own because it took up a growing amount of his thinking time.

His big question to me was, "Can Jesus really break the sexual bondage of pornography that I am in?" Of course the answer is "Yes," but I don't know any "quick fix." Achieving freedom will necessitate great perseverance and godly choices as well as the power of Jesus to break every chain of the enemy. We will consider how to break these bondages later on.

My strong counsel, especially to men, is to be vigilant over sexual sin and pornography. Do not even look at the soft stuff and disable your computer if necessary. Once you know that you are vulnerable, do not have satellite TV which shows late-night adult erotica and worse. Make a vow to God in front of your wife that pornography will in no way feature in your life. Agree to be accountable to someone you can trust to keep you on track.

Every servant of God must have clean hands and a clean heart. Sexual integrity is a must and the enemy has declared "WAR"! This will be a battle for most men. Whilst pornography is mostly a male issue, it is not exclusively so and more and more women are getting involved with such things as parties with male strippers.

Masturbation

Some Christian books will teach that masturbation is all right and perfectly normal, but from my experience I have seen otherwise. The spirit of masturbation has an appetite for masturbation and not sexual intercourse. The popular deception is that when we cannot have sex, we masturbate to "relieve" ourselves.

I prayed with a woman who had had a problem with masturbation since she was a five-year-old. She became involved with multiple sexual partners and she told me that even when she had sex several times a day, she still had to masturbate several times a day too and she could not understand why.

There is a spirit behind masturbation, which makes it another very addictive habit. It is impossible to masturbate without fantasizing or to control what comes down the fantasy tube into the mind. Masturbation is, of course, often fuelled by pornography and allows the human spirit to be penetrated by defiling and unclean spirits when these things are entered into.

Masturbation begins as false comfort. It is an attempt to bring comfort from deep inner pain and feelings of rejection and inadequacy. A person may masturbate when they feel bad on the inside and it can be a soulish way of dealing with loneliness and isolation. It is also a form of self-idolatry.

Lack of recognition of their own need for inner healing or lack of understanding of the role of the Holy Spirit as the Comforter, may be the reason why many Christians seek the false comfort that comes through masturbation. They may justify their practice by believing the popular deception that masturbation is a legitimate method of relieving built-up sexual feelings when intercourse is not an option.

Why would Spirit-filled believers want false comfort when they have the Holy Spirit, the true Comforter as promised by

Jesus (John 14:16)? The word "Comforter" comes from the Latin *confortare* meaning to "strengthen from the inside." God will give the Holy Spirit to fill and touch the places of deep inner pain and bring true comfort and strength. Sometimes even though a believer moves in the gifts of the Holy Spirit they know nothing of the Holy Spirit as Comforter.

Root causes

It is not normal for a child to enter into sexual behavior before puberty, unless their sexuality has been wrongly awakened. When a person has had a sexual addiction or problem long before puberty it could well be an outworking of sexual sin on the generational line. Alternatively, it might be as a result of some form of sexual abuse and the transfer of an unclean spirit.

The tie with the abuser will very often be the enemy's foot-hold or channel into the child's spirit. It is not uncommon for victims of childhood sexual abuse to struggle with masturbation problems. Frequently abusers teach children masturbatory sex and mutual masturbation takes place, as a result of which a spirit/demon can transfer into the child.

Another reason for masturbation in children before adolescence can be the absence of a mother's love (in either male or female children). Children trying to deal with deep separation anxiety clutch at their genitals to try and find comfort. If they cannot get parental attention healthily, they will try unhealthy ways. The genitals are very sensitive to touch and these children desperately need to be touched. There is a bodily tenseness. They could also rock, or rub their arm continuously or there may be a need to touch their hair. Masturbation can temporarily relieve the pain but often it leads to addictive and destructive behavior, guilt and shame.

Deep emotional pain can produce genital pressure. Like an emergency alert the body's alarm system goes off, which says: "I have deep unmet needs. Others who should be meeting them are not; therefore I need to meet them myself."

The spirit of masturbation wants masturbation and nothing

else, and is not satisfied by sexual intercourse. The solution, of course, is not just to deliver the person of the demon. We must do that, but wherever there is a demon there will be the need for deep inner healing and wholeness too. Remembering sex is not just physical we will need to bring healing to the human spirit as well as the deep inner emotional pain. The question to be answered is: "What is the root cause of masturbation?"

A pastor was arrested for pedophilia and in complete personal disbelief and devastation came with his wife for help. I asked him to tell us his story from the beginning. He and his wife no longer shared a bed and had become emotionally separate. He found that when he felt "low," he would lie on his bed and masturbate and it made the inner pain go away for a short while. He felt ashamed as this habit became more regular and more intense. One day at a ministers' fraternal the question was asked, "Is it all right for us as Christians to masturbate, especially when our wives no longer adequately meet all our sexual needs?" Everyone replied, "Of course it is, we all do it and it doesn't hurt anyone."

Following that fraternal meeting he felt released from guilt, and began to masturbate frequently. He started to find that the fantasies were of young girls and gradually they became younger and younger until they were children. On the fateful day, he was masturbating and fantasizing. The child was about five years old. She wore a pink dress, had golden hair, blue eyes, white socks and patent shoes, and as he fantasized he had masturbatory sex with her. Afterwards he went downstairs to make himself a cup of coffee and in the kitchen, to his complete amazement, stood the little girl he had seen in his fantasy.

Emily was five years old and her mother had a hospital appointment that day. The pastor's wife had agreed to look after Emily. He said to his wife: "You wanted to change your library books this morning; why don't you do that and I'll look after Emily?" He took Emily by the hand and took her upstairs and did exactly what he had done in his fantasy.

The police were called and they arrested and charged him. He said: "Please believe me. I am not a pedophile. I have never done anything like this before – please help me – it all started with masturbation." It is a very small step between fantasizing and doing it in reality. All temptation begins in the mind and that is the battleground where we must gain the victory.

Telephone sex/cybersex

In recent years there has been an explosion in the availability of so-called telephone sex. Initially this involved chat rooms where women were paid to keep men on the telephone line at extortionate call rates with dirty sexual talk. Often the men masturbate and become addicted very quickly. None of this is actually illegal in the UK and the USA.

Telephone sex has now expanded to include women callers as well as men, and there are also gay sex telephone lines and groups "talking dirty" together. Mobile phones make all of this very available to all, including children. People can become addicted and spend huge sums on telephone sex where rates per minute are expensive. Since mobile phones now have Internet connection, pornography websites are even easier to access and the fact that "pay as you go" services do not generally require people to register by name, makes it possible to view pornography without being traced.

The Internet has opened up readily available "fantasy lust" and masturbatory sexual opportunities. In combination with web cameras and electronically controlled so-called "sex aids" and body sensors, possibilities now exist for defiling, mutual, remote sexual expression with same- or opposite-sex partners who may even be complete strangers.

Voyeurism

Voyeurism is where someone gets their "kicks" from watching others have sex. TV, videos and films have in many aspects made voyeurs of us all. Believers need to be increasingly selective about what they watch. Very defiling visual images, once taken in, can be re-played in the mind or relayed into dreams. It is easy to watch a film, not suspecting it to contain explicit sexual scenes and get hooked by the storyline and "sit through" the sexual scenes in order to know how the story ends. These films usually contain sexual swear words too and so our thoughts and mind can be defiled by what we see or hear.

> ... *whatsoever things are pure, whatsoever things are lovely, whatsoever things are of good report ... think on these things.*
> (Philippians 4:8 KJV)

Voyeurs watch from a distance and only experience intimacy at a distance. Their sexuality is only awakened by observing that to which they cannot relate face to face.

Bestiality

Bestiality is having sex with animals. Leviticus 18:23 says:

> "*Do not have sexual relations with an animal and defile yourself with it. A woman must not present herself to an animal to have sexual relations with it; that is a perversion.*"

Sex with animals can bring heavy demonization: remember we are "one" with everyone/thing we have sex with. This will establish an ungodly soul-tie between a human being and the animal. I would expect that anyone desiring or tempted to have sex with an animal probably has bestiality and/or high-powered occult sin on their generational line. Bestiality is not uncommon with family pets.

In South Africa, where there is a major AIDS epidemic, I was told of men (not Christians) who keep goats specifically for the purpose of bestiality. This is rooted in the belief that having sex with human beings makes them vulnerable to AIDS but having sex with animals does not. Speaking about Satan, Jesus said,

> *"When he lies, he speaks his native language, for he is a liar and the father of lies."*

(John 8:44)

They may not get AIDS but they will get something spiritually far worse. I was also told that the fetish priests (occultists/ witch-doctors) have declared that having sex with a baby cleanses a man from the AIDS virus. This has greatly increased the incidence of sex with babies and small children.

Godly Expression of Sexuality

Having looked at many ways in which the enemy sets a trap and causes people to express their sexuality wrongly, it would be good to remind ourselves of the beautiful truths of God's Word. Let us look at the rightful and godly expression of sexuality within the secure boundaries of a loving marriage relationship.

God's way is for our good and our blessing; He does not wish to constrict us, but to give to us abundant life now and eternal life to come. God's intention is that married couples are firstly in a covenant relationship with Him through Jesus and then, secondly, in their covenant relationship of marriage together. There is no competition in these two relationships, however. The second one flows naturally from the first one.

Godly order

When a husband takes up his rightful headship, he loves his wife and family and spends quality time with them as a priority. Most of the decisions the couple face should be made together and only when no agreement can be found should the husband's decision be final. Husband and wife are one in flesh and spirit in God's sight and, when they are in godly order, they model Christian marriage as God intended.

Unlike animals, we are made in God's image and we are eternal beings into which God has breathed His Spirit. What God is, His essential God-ness, He breathed into man. We are the pinnacles of God's creation and He gave us the ability to reproduce offspring who are also eternal beings. Human beings are creative, bringing into existence many new things, but perhaps the highest act of creativity they are capable of is the ability to bring children into the world. We call this "procreation," a word which really means creation "on behalf of" God. In bringing new life into being we are reflecting God as Creator.

The wife and husband should respect each other and model this in their behavior to the children. A wife should particularly encourage the children to respect and obey their father. God intends children to grow up under the strong protection and blessing of a loving, stable covenant of marriage between a mum and dad who, in love together, bring their children up in the Lord. It is then a family where the primary relationship is with Jesus Christ and God the Father through the power of the Holy Spirit.

The children are being trained and disciplined to come under the spiritual protection and authority of their parents and not to rebel against godly order. This is the path of blessing for the human family. The author James Dobson teaches that we should bring our children up with a moral conscience that is obedient to parents without asking "why?"[1]

What amazing changes would take place if everyone in our street, our city and our country lived like that! The family is after all the core unit of the nations of the world.

Role of the husband

The husband's role is to be the head of the marriage. In Ephesians 5:23 Paul writes,

For the husband is the head of the wife as Christ is the head of the church . . .

(Ephesians 5:23)

He is the leader. He holds the spiritual covering over his wife and family. He is called to be the provider and the protector, even to the laying down of his own life. Husbands are called to love their wives as they love themselves and in the same way as Christ loved the Church and gave His life for the Church (Ephesians 5:32). This is indeed a high calling for husbands.

Role of the wife

A wife is called to "submit" to her husband (Ephesians 5:24). This means to walk in harmony with her husband; to be his helper, supporter and encourager; always to think well of him; always to love him. A wife needs to encourage her husband to lead. She needs to accept and submit to his authority. Wives are most fulfilled and most secure underneath the spiritual covering of their husbands.

It is the wife's role to choose to submit to her husband because this is right before God – a husband cannot insist on her submission. Submission is initiated by the wife. Submission is always initiated by the person doing the submitting. When God created Eve He called her a "helpmeet" or a "counterpart." Many wives seem to feel inferior to their husbands but that is not how God views them.

We have seen that God has created each one of us to need significance, security and self-worth. In the Bible we see the apostle Paul exhorting wives to respect their husbands. His emphasis indicates that men have a greater need for significance, so a good wife tries to ensure that she always makes her husband feel significant. Husbands are told to love their wives, laying down their lives for them. This is recognition that a wife has a greater need to feel secure, safe and protected.

A good husband tries to ensure she always feels safe in his arms.

The wonder and beauty of sex within marriage

In the beginning, before the Fall, Adam and Eve were able to enjoy a close, intimate relationship with nothing to spoil it whatsoever:

> *The man and his wife were both naked, and they felt no shame.*
>
> (Genesis 2:25)

God still intends married couples to have joy and pleasure in their relationship. Blessings come down godly soul-ties. In Proverbs 5:18–19 we read:

> *May your fountain be blessed,*
>   *and may you rejoice in the wife of your youth.*
> *A loving doe, a graceful deer –*
>   *may her breasts satisfy you always,*
>   *may you ever be captivated by her love.*

Godly sexual intercourse is in itself creative because it feeds and nurtures the spirit, and sexual relations are expected to continue throughout the marriage. Nurture is creative because it brings about something that did not exist before – building and restoring.

That again is why Paul instructs husbands and wives not to deprive each other of the physical pleasure and satisfaction of regular sexual relations. The only activity that is to break it is prayer and fasting for some specific cause, and this is to be only by mutual consent for a very limited time.

> *The husband should fulfill his marital duty to his wife, and likewise the wife to her husband. The wife's body does not belong to her alone but also to her husband. In the same way, the*

husband's body does not belong to him alone but also to his wife. Do not deprive each other except by mutual consent and for a time, so that you may devote yourselves to prayer. Then come together again so that Satan will not tempt you because of your lack of self-control.

(1 Corinthians 7:3–5)

The marriage bed is a holy place in the sight of God and we should be careful to maintain this viewpoint ourselves:

Marriage should be honored by all, and the marriage bed kept pure, for God will judge the adulterer and all the sexually immoral.

(Hebrews 13:4)

I have already made reference to the fact that men and women are "wired up" differently physically and sexually, and are aroused sexually in different ways. Men have a visual sexual response and drive – that is, they are "turned on" by what they see. They might only regard sexual intercourse as a means of quick fulfillment for themselves but then their wives may feel they are just being used as an object, only wanted for their body and not loved as a person. Husbands need to learn not to rush into lovemaking but to take time to arouse passion in their wives and make sure they are blessed. The Bible instructs that, particularly in the first year of marriage, a husband should make his wife's happiness his priority:

If a man has recently married, he must not be sent to war or have any other duty laid on him. For one year he is free to stay at home and bring happiness to the wife he has married.

(Deuteronomy 24:5)

For women sexual intercourse is only a part of expressing love in the whole of the marriage relationship. What happens during the day is as important as what happens at night in bed.

A wife needs emotional nurture and continual love and care. Women are "turned on" by speech and touch. One of the most effective ways a husband can show his love for his wife is by speaking words of tenderness and affection.

In the Bible we can find many tender expressions of love in the poetry of the Song of Songs, for example:

> How delightful is your love, my sister, my bride!
>   How much more pleasing is your love than wine,
>   and the fragrance of your perfume than any spice!
> Your lips drop sweetness as the honeycomb, my bride;
>   milk and honey are under your tongue.
>   The fragrance of your garments is like that of Lebanon.
> You are a garden locked up, my sister, my bride;
>   you are a spring enclosed, a sealed fountain.
>
> (4:10–12)

King Solomon calls his wife a garden enclosed and she responds by saying,

> Awake, north wind,
>   and come, south wind!
> Blow on my garden,
>   that its fragrance may spread abroad.
> Let my lover come into his garden
>   and taste its choice fruits.
>
> (4:16)

Physical touch is very important in marriage to both men and women, but for women it is a primary arouser. Touch receptors are located throughout the body. These tiny tactile areas are not scattered evenly but arranged in clusters. The tip of the tongue is highly sensitive, as are the tips of the fingers, the tip of the nose and of course our genitalia. The back of the shoulders is one of the least sensitive areas.

It is important to convey love by holding hands, kissing,

cuddling and embracing. Sometimes, just putting a hand on the other one's shoulder shows support. Hugs are not only for giving a message of passion but also affection and security. Women like them to be given often without an expectation that they will always lead to sexual intercourse. Women want their husbands to tell them constantly that they are loved and hold them. It is very important for a husband to hold his wife, especially when she cries. Being hugged in a time of crisis is a powerful communicator of love.

We cannot always change events but we can survive if we feel loved. Tender touches will be remembered long after the crisis has passed. Gary Chapman in his book *The Five Love Languages* says: "Whatever there is of me resides in my body. To touch my body is to touch me."[2]

In the next chapter we will look at some more ways in which the enemy has deceived us by distorting the wonderful gift of sexuality and how God's heart is to bring healing and restoration.

Notes

1. *Dare to Discipline* (Tyndale House Pub., 1977, repr. 1992).
2. Northfield Publishers, 1995.

Deceived by the Enemy

Deception and lies are the major tools of our enemy Satan. Jesus, in describing him, said: *"he is a liar and the father of lies"* (John 8:44). Many people today are confused about their sexual identity and the expression of their sexuality because they have believed the lies of the enemy and are deceived in their thinking. The lies they have believed and the denial of God's truth have led many into deceptive lifestyles and an expression of their sexuality which dishonors God. In this chapter we will look at some of the issues that arise from the deception of the enemy.

God's unchangeable Word

God has created mankind as heterosexual; all other sexual orientations are contrary to His creation ordinances and against His will. A person's God-given sexual identity and gender is revealed by their genital organs rather than their thoughts and emotions. There are those today who claim that they are really a man in a woman's body or vice versa. They do not accept the sexual identity given to them and claim to have a sexual attraction or an orientation towards the same sex.

Andrew Cominskey, in his book *The Kingdom of God and the Homosexual*,[1] says,

Homosexual tendencies are powerful feelings of sexual and emotional attraction that one has for the same sex. The long-standing nature of these tendencies is the key to determining whether one is actually dealing with a same sex attraction or not.

He goes on to say:

There is a difference between those who have persistent tendencies from childhood or teen years and those who experiment bi-sexually now and again in a very promiscuous culture.

There are obviously some differences with regard to how seriously a person's sexual orientation has been affected. However, if a person gets a sexual arousal from looking at someone of the same sex, and fantasizes about having a sexual relationship, even without physical touch of any sort, a problem exists.

It certainly cannot be denied that homosexuality is one of the "hot potatoes" confronting the Body of Christ today. I believe passionately that, as the Church is intended to be Christ's Body, with Christ as its head, it must proclaim the truth that is in Christ and the Word of God. It should not vary its teaching to compromise with political correctness.

Jesus never compromised in His bold teaching of truth, nor was He ever in fear of the political leaders not agreeing with Him. We read that when some Pharisees came to Jesus telling Him to leave because Herod wanted to kill Him, Jesus replied,

"Go tell that fox, 'I will drive out demons and heal people today and tomorrow, and on the third day I will reach my goal.'"
(Luke 13:32)

He was not intimidated or caused to change His plans even by death threats from one of the most powerful men around. In teaching what God's Word says we are not merely giving our opinion – it is the unchangeable, eternal truth of God.

Leviticus 18:22 says:

> *"Do not lie with a man as one lies with a woman; that is detestable."*

Likewise in Romans 1:27 we read,

> *In the same way the men also abandoned natural relations with women and were inflamed with lust for one another. Men committed indecent acts with other men, and received in themselves the due penalty for their perversion.*

The Old and New Testaments both teach that homosexual behavior is sinful and against God's will. However, God loves the person who has homosexual confusion, even though He hates the sin he or she is committing. As Christians we are commanded to love and value others and yet hate sin of every kind. Our acceptance of others is to be unconditional even though we cannot approve of sinful behavior. We are also obliged to speak God's Word into all situations and be a prophetic voice to the world.

Confusion in the Church

Unfortunately, churches who ordain homosexuals and lesbians are approving of those who practice sin. When church leaders are allowed to continue the practice of homosexuality and still be in spiritual authority over their church, their spiritual covering over their flock will be damaged in that area, and the same sins will start to be found throughout that church.

> *Although they know God's righteous decree that those who do such things deserve death, they not only continue to do these very things but also approve of those who practice them.*
>
> (Romans 1:32)

Recently, when I was praying about the ordination of homosexual bishops, I sensed God showing me that in the Body
of Christ it is as if there are three circles, each indicating a
certain level of commitment to Jesus Christ. The first circle is
the "outer court" or the nominal Christians. The second is the
"inner court" of the established Church with a form of religious
faith, and the third is the Holy of Holies. The Holy of Holies is
representative of active, born-again, Spirit-filled believers who
are obedient to the call of God on their lives. Satan is not
content with the outer court, but is headed for the Holy of
Holies. Let us be very alert to Satan's devices and never be
complacent and think it could not affect us!

Some groups want to remove all restrictions to homosexuality. Many are now very forthright and open about their
sexuality including all aspects of homosexuality and lesbianism.
There is a huge pull in our culture to affirm people in this
orientation and behavior. Therefore the Spirit-filled Body of
Christ cannot afford to be silent. Evil triumphs when good
people do nothing. We need to give a clear "trumpet call" into
our world and a clear proclamation about what the Bible
teaches.

If all restrictions were to be removed I believe that the
activity of child abusers would increase and bring destruction to
the lives of children, many of whom are already vulnerable
because of being tempted into drug addiction. I believe it would
also result in increased idolatry bringing the righteous judgment of God. Such consequences were seen in the Bible in
Genesis 19 when catastrophe fell on Sodom and Gomorrah as a
judgment for such behavior.

Rather than affirming homosexual and lesbian lifestyles,
believers should help those who want to be living a life which
pleases God but who struggle in this area. No matter what our
sin, Jesus offers to each one of us the way to healing through
repentance and forgiveness. A climate of love and acceptance
makes it easier for sinners to humble themselves and be open
with their church leaders about their problem. They will not be

held back by fear of condemnation. Ministry should be offered
to them which is appropriate and which is motivated by
genuine love.

Root causes of homosexual confusion

A dysfunctional home with an absentee or emotionally remote
father is one of the common platforms for homosexual
confusion. Where are the strong fathers? Are they heading up
their families under God? Are they being priests in their own
homes? Often the fathers are very weak themselves and
emotionally detached from their children or absent altogether.
This causes rejection in the child who may then conclude that
he or she is a disappointment in some way.

Maybe boys feel they should have been girls, and girls that
they should have been boys. A boy can also have a "smother-
ing" mother who fusses over him too much, which results in
his peer group considering him to be "a mummy's boy" or a
weakling. This in turn fosters yet more rejection. He longs for
his father to love and affirm him, but it never happens.

Frequently generational sin gives the demonic rights. There
is a spirit of homosexuality that simply uses a person's body to
get its homosexual appetites met. Demons are disembodied
spirits who need a body to work through. I believe that people
can be occupied by homosexual or lesbian spirits and these
spirits could have been there since conception, or birth, or
given a place early in childhood. These spirits can be transferred
through abuse or through an ungodly soul-tie. People will say
things like: "You know, long before puberty I knew I was gay –
I was always different." In the spiritual dimensions they are
simply saying: "I was occupied by this demon very early on."

Separation anxiety is often a major root, which can lead to a
person hating the parent who did not connect with them and
cause them to open themselves up to others in a way that is
completely inappropriate.

We have seen that sexual expression involves our human
spirit. But when a person's human spirit becomes crushed and

broken through damage, usually in the formative years of development, the functions of that human spirit can become distorted and broken. There can be a core identity disorder which will have an outworking in the sexual area. People with homosexual confusion often suffer from rejection of their sexuality. For many the root cause is that they never had their sexual identity affirmed by their parents.

All boys need to be brought up as boys. They need their father to take them to do things that men do: go to a football match, build a bonfire together in the garden or fix the car together; they need their father to say, "I am so glad that you are my son and I love you for who you are."

For many men, father never hugged them and never taught them about being men and how to treat women properly. Today, in the west, so many of our boys are brought up in broken homes. Single-parent families have doubled in the United Kingdom in the last ten years, and most children of broken marriages have been brought up by mothers on their own. They are then taught by lady teachers and if they only have a sister, there can be no male input at all into their lives. They may have been put in the bath with their sister and, through shortage of space in housing, they may also have shared a bedroom (if not a bed). This lack of sexual identity is compounded by the unisex dressing of contemporary culture. As a result the formative development of many boys is very far from that which God intended.

Born the "wrong" sex – George's story

I conducted a long-term ministry for over two years with a boy who suffered from schizophrenia. His mother had wanted a girl and when George was born she had prepared only pink clothing. Although he was "George – boy" on his birth certificate she called him "Georgina" and dressed him totally as a girl and presented him as such. By the age of five he went to school dressed as a girl. Mother withdrew him from all games and gym saying he had a weak heart and strongly instructed George never to undress in front of anyone. He went right through his junior school until he was eleven years old, dressed as a girl. His father had left home and George's true gender had been denied and never affirmed.

That summer, mother and her sister, George's auntie, took him to a holiday camp. His hair was in long blonde curls. He had blue eyes. On the Friday night there was a "Prettiest Little Girl" competition and mother and auntie entered George "for a laugh." They dressed him in a frilly dress. Mother and auntie got rather drunk that night and of course George won, to be met with absolutely hysterical drunken laughter by mother and auntie. To think they had pulled this off and "conned" the judges into believing George was a little girl was a highlight moment for them.

That night something inside George broke and he ran for his life. He went to an Oxfam shop and bought himself some jeans and a T-shirt and ripped off his girl's clothes, cut off his own hair on the beach and made a vow that he would never return home. He never did. He was nearly twelve when he hit the streets and it wasn't long before he fell victim to an old homosexual predator who took him in and George became a homosexual too.

I was asked to visit George in a psychiatric ward in St Thomas' Hospital, London. George had lived a "double role" all of his formative years, knowing he was male but having to present himself as female – not surprisingly he was diagnosed as schizophrenic. I led George to the Lord on the floor of the psychiatric ward and saw God profoundly move into his life. I am always amazed at the great lengths to which Jesus will go for one damaged and broken lamb.

The next day I was in the office and the receptionist rang up to say I had a visitor. I went down to see George with a small bag containing his belongings. "I told my psychiatrist I'm healed. Jesus has saved me! So they let me go and I am going to live with you!" So George moved in for a few days until we found proper accommodation for him and he joined our

church. I wish I could say, "And we lived happily ever after ..."
George was a challenge to us all and we saw God transform his
life in many areas. George would take his medication for a
while and be really stable and then announce he was healed so
he didn't need to take it any more! Gradually he would become
mentally unstable and confused and would need psychiatric
help again. We learned to love him, even when he would be
drawn back to the "bright lights" of London and the "gay bars"
and would then come back in guilt and remorse.

It was a hard slog for George to get free and to maintain that
freedom. But I knew that Jesus Christ is still the *only* one
that can put back what is missing in the core identity and heal
the human spirit of all the damage and inner brokenness.

George would tell me he could go to an unknown town and
get off the train, turn left and then turn right round the corner
into the only "gay bar" in town. He said: "It is like a homing
pigeon's instinct." What really happens, of course, is that the
homosexual spirit in him networks with the ruling homosexual
spirits over the town and guides him to the place where they
can get their appetites met. George's mother probably had little
awareness of the impact on George of what she was doing. It
was in direct rebellion against God. We must agree with God
that He is right and that He doesn't make mistakes. We need to
accept our own gender and that of our children as God's plan
and submit joyfully to it; otherwise the consequences can be
disastrous.

Other causes of homosexual confusion

Homosexual confusion can have its roots in experimentation at
school. When we go through puberty we are discovering our
bodies and what they are capable of sexually. To get involved in
some experimentation does not mean a person will develop a
same-sex orientation in the future, but of course the enemy will
be able to gain rights in that person's life.

Abuse in early childhood by someone of the same sex can
cause a homosexual spirit to come down the ungodly soul-tie.

Sometimes I have heard a person who is saved and has had homosexual confusion in the past say, "If I don't practice homosexual behavior, is that all right?" I want to say, "Why have a life's struggle against all those powers of darkness when you could be free!" *"If the Son sets you free, you will be free indeed!"* (John 8:36).

Confusion of sexual orientation in women

The Bible mentions that women can have a problem with confusion in expressing their sexuality: *"Even their women exchanged natural relations for unnatural ones"* (Romans 1:26b). In modern terms we normally refer to a homosexual orientation and behavior in women as lesbianism. The distinguishing feature for women is emotional intensity. These relationships can become very heavy, very exclusive and very claustrophobic and physical. It has been described as "a relationship addiction between women that is eroticized."

Possible causes could be that a girl does not receive proper nurture, that is love, encouragement, affirmation, safety to fail, protection and significance from her mother, and therefore becomes susceptible. If her mother was told, "You have a baby girl," and she responded, "Oh no! Not a girl!", then somewhere deep in the human spirit of the baby, rejection of her gender was registered. Maybe she began to feel she should have been a boy, that there is something intrinsically wrong with her and somewhere deep in her psyche she tries to make up for that through her behavior. Babies receive messages through their human spirits because their mental development and understanding is only just beginning.

As a result of this rejection a girl can become emotionally detached from her mother. This could be a conscious decision to "pull the plug" on her relationship with her mother or it might be unconscious at a deeper level within her. She feels she is not able to depend on her mother who will not look after her or protect her. She concludes that if she's going to survive she will have to do it by herself.

This will happen before puberty and she may pull away from being kissed or hugged by mother. She can develop "loner" activities, spending much time on her own in her bedroom, or walking or cycling alone, or maybe she has a pony or a pet that she dotes upon. Gradually a same-sex attraction develops in her which is not sexual at this stage. She may have a crush on the gym mistress or an older woman who shows her attention. There is something inside her which is losing out on the love of mother, and she is unconsciously looking to make up the deficit.

An adopted girl who cannot come to terms with the fact that her birth mother did not love her enough to keep her, may also have this response. I have prayed with middle-aged women who are still agonizing over the question, "How could the mother who gave me life, put me out for adoption?" It is the ultimate abandonment and for many the pain goes very, very deep. They often develop anger about it which results in a real "chip on their shoulder" and major rejection, sometimes for the whole of life.

I recently prayed with a lady who was not told by her adopted parents that she was adopted. She did not find out until she went to the passport office to apply for a passport. She was asked to transfer to a different section where a secular counselor was waiting to tell her that her parents were not her birth parents. It came as a huge shock to her as an adult.

If a young girl is abused by her father and mother turns a "blind eye," then this will engender a hatred towards mother and the belief in her that her mother cannot be trusted with her emotional needs. If as a young girl she tried to tell her mother what was going on at night and mother exploded angrily, accusing her of lying, this can be a contributory factor in the pull towards lesbian behavior.

As she reaches puberty she is not looking for an opposite sex relationship, she is looking for a same-sex relationship, to make up for the loss of true mother love. She wants to matter to somebody, to be more important than anybody else in that person's life. She is looking for her own deep unmet emotional needs to be met. She wants to be mothered, but the worst thing you could say to her would be, "Aren't you so like your mother!"

As she moves from relationship to relationship because of her rejection, the relationships are rarely sustained and become overtly sexual and erotic. This can mask the real reason of her confusion. Her orientation towards other women is not so much about sex, but is all about looking for emotional affirmation, encouragement and significance – those vital ingredients that were left out of her formative development. By now she probably believes the lie "I am a lesbian – that is my identity."

Healing for men and women in sexual brokenness and confusion

There is hope and freedom for those who struggle in the area of sexual brokenness and confusion. Sexual wholeness comes when we are in God's truth and in covenant relationship with Him. Experiencing the "Father heart of God" will be a very deep and precious gateway to this healing. Jesus said we are to come to God the Father through Him. He is "the Way, the Truth and the Life" (John 14:6).

All our sexuality, and its expression, is to be under the Lordship of Jesus Christ. In other words all our life, including our sexual behavior, is to be an act of worship to God, as we live in obedience to His Word. Healing can only take place in this context.

God's truth will need to replace all the lies planted by the enemy. A paradigm shift in beliefs is needed before any change or healing can be received. I teach God's truth and challenge men and women to disbelieve the "gay" propaganda, which says: "You are a homosexual or a lesbian. That is your identity; you cannot change that, so accept it and enjoy life."

Much damage comes out of these lies which Satan is speaking through various mouthpieces and which sound convincing.

Believing these lies results in a passive and hopeless acceptance that nothing could ever change and destroys faith in God's healing transforming power. I always try and discourage a person from using labels about their core identity such as "I am an alcoholic" or "I am a homosexual." I tell them, "No, you are not. At the moment you are suffering from alcoholism or homosexual confusion. We pray that Jesus will heal you."

I want to take you to the Word of God which affirms that there is full healing and wholeness for the repentant homosexual:

> *Do you not know that the wicked will not inherit the kingdom of God? Do not be deceived: Neither the sexually immoral nor idolaters nor adulterers nor male prostitutes nor homosexual offenders nor thieves nor the greedy nor drunkards nor slanderers nor swindlers will inherit the kingdom of God. And that is what some of you were. But you were washed, you were sanctified, you were justified in the name of the Lord Jesus Christ and by the Spirit of our God.*
>
> (1 Corinthians 6:9–11)

It is so wonderfully encouraging to find out that in the early Corinthian church there was cleansing and sanctification for all kinds of sinners in the name of the Lord Jesus Christ and by the Spirit of our God.

Once a strong faith and trust in Jesus is established, like a rock and foundation, the way is then open to receive healing and deliverance. Although the root causes of emotional pain need to be understood, healing begins with deep repentance and a willingness to renounce the wrong lifestyle completely.

Following repentance, the breaking of ungodly soul-ties with abusers and sexual partners will need to take place so that there can be prayer for deliverance.

When we were asking Jesus to cut George's ungodly soul-ties we learned to do it by the year, as he had no memory of how many relationships he had had or whom they were with. I realized the importance of cutting him free because each of his sexual partners was likely to have had multiple sexual partners too. I know that Satan's strategy is to link together and control people through the ungodly soul-ties which they have formed.

In addition to deliverance from demonic spirits there will need to be prayer asking God to heal the brokenness in the human spirit and to restore the core identity of the person. Confirmation and affirmation of their sexual identity from God as their heavenly Father is so important. Many have never been parented in any real sense by their earthly parents and God often uses the ministry team as godly role models of fathers and mothers in a deep process of inner healing.

Bisexuality

Another area of sexual brokenness and confusion is when people believe that they can just as easily be both heterosexual and homosexual or lesbian in their sexual orientation. Married men have sexual relationships with other men and married women have sexual relationships with other women. I believe they have been deceived by the enemy, are suffering deep confusion and have a core identity disorder. They have difficulty in answering the question "Who am I?" Often they say they are bisexual because they want to please both the gays and the heterosexuals, believing they can "flip flop" between sexual orientations.

Transvestism

Some people begin dressing in the clothes of the opposite sex to obtain sexual arousal and stimulation (normally described as transvestites). This would normally involve masturbation. They are mostly men but by no means exclusively so.

A man may have begun obtaining sexual arousal through wearing women's lingerie and shaving his legs and wearing stockings, high-heeled shoes and make-up. I prayed with a

Christian woman in Sweden who came home early one evening to find her husband dressed in her underwear with make-up on and masturbating. It was a huge shock for her but actually a relief for him that it was no longer a guilty secret.

Cross-dressing

Some people dress in the clothes of the opposite sex because of huge gender confusion and because they are rejecting the gender that God created for them to be. Cross-dressing may be more than secretive activities at home and may involve wearing the clothes of the opposite sex in public. Women's clothes in men's sizes can be bought from trans-sexual catalogues. Such behavior is an attempt to change one's sexual identity and have that identity recognized by others.

A cross-dresser may gain security by wearing women's clothes. Comfort from clothes can become a replacement for a mother and an attempt to fill the void created as a result of not having received mother love. Those who behave in this way have a need for inner healing and need to find their true security in Jesus.

Transsexuality

A cross-dresser whose feelings become progressively stronger may eventually believe, "I am a woman trapped in a man's body," which causes a desire to have plastic surgery to remove his genitalia and to have an artificial vagina made. He will need to take huge amounts of hormones to deal with his male voice and facial hair and may undergo breast implant surgery. He may now want to change his name by deed poll and present himself as a woman.

There was a case in the newspapers of a man who was a vicar in the Church of England. He had a sex-change operation and returned to the same parish as a female vicar! Another story about a sex-change operation came into the public arena when there was outrage from some parents at a well-known private co-educational boarding school. A male teacher changed his sex and came back to the school as a woman. He was a father of two and his wife of twenty-seven years was said to have decided to stay in the marriage!

Under the Sex Discrimination Act (Gender Reassignment Regulations 1999) he was entitled not to suffer any detriment or discrimination by reason of his change of sex. There was a paper sent to the parents written by an "expert" who stressed that the teacher's condition, known as "Gender Dysphasia" or "Gender Identification Disorder," has nothing to do with homosexuality or pedophilia.

A national television channel in the UK aired a program called *Make Me a Man*, documenting the stories of four women following their quest to become men. Now called Scott, Stephen, Lee and Bob they had mastectomies on both breasts, large daily amounts of hormones and plastic male genitalia added. One of the women (now presenting as a man) had married a woman and they had adopted children, who called "her" Daddy.

To reject our God-given gender in such radical ways is blatant rebellion against godly order. The sadness is that the deep inner emotional pain and rejection, from which these people are suffering, is of course not healed by a sex change and they carry their baggage with them into their new identity. Afterwards disillusionment and hopelessness can set in, sometimes leading to suicide.

One day I was telephoned by a church leader who told me that a transsexual had come to Christ through Alpha, and they were keen to disciple her (previously him). What was our counsel over the sex change? Now that "he" had changed to "she," was it all right for that to continue? I am sure he did not want to hear my reply. Jesus *"gave himself for us to redeem us from all wickedness"* (Titus 2:14), not to leave us in our sins. The new Christian needs to agree with God that He was right to make him a man and repent and turn back to become the man He intended him to be.

The ministry of healing for such confusion will involve deep inner healing of emotional pain and brokenness in the human spirit. Only Jesus Christ can bring this person into permanent healing and freedom.

Summary

God loves those who are sexually broken, confused and struggle with their sexual identity. However, they need to recognize that their behavior is ungodly and repent and turn from it. There will be a need for inner healing ministry and deliverance. They will need to be re-taught many truths and they must be willing to change their core beliefs about who they are in Christ. With regard to those who are unrepentant about their homosexual or lesbian behavior, the Bible is very straightforward:

> *They exchanged the truth of God for a lie, and worshiped and served created things rather than the Creator . . .*
>
> (Romans 1:25)

> *But among you there must not be even a hint of sexual immorality . . . these are improper for God's holy people . . . For of this you can be sure: No immoral, impure or greedy person – such a man is an idolater – has any inheritance in the kingdom of Christ and of God. Let no one deceive you with empty words, for because of such things God's wrath comes on those who are disobedient. Therefore do not be partners with them.*
>
> (Ephesians 5:3, 5 – 7)

It is essential that people who have been caught in a homosexual or lesbian lifestyle know that they are loved unconditionally. It is equally important, though, that they should choose to live their life according to the scriptural norm.

Note

1. Available from Desert Stream Ministries, PO Box 9999, Kansas City, MO 64134, USA; email: info@desertstream.org.

Defiled by the Enemy

We have seen how God created sex to be a beautiful expression of a loving relationship within the security of the marriage covenant. Sadly the entry of sin into the world has meant that some have abused the gift of sex and have forced sexual intercourse upon others against their will. In Leviticus chapter 18 sexual abuse is included amongst those sexual practices which are an abomination to God. It defiles those involved in it and even the land itself. God warned His people not to let themselves be defiled in this way, explaining in detail what sexual practices were to be avoided.

Sexual abuse can be defined as expressing sexuality against the will of another individual or where sexual expression is not appropriate to the age or psychological state of that other person. The victims of sexual abuse can suffer tremendous inner damage and defilement because of what has happened. They will feel violated and unclean. They often feel confused about their own identity and falsely feel that they somehow were partly responsible for what happened. They will need inner healing and deliverance as a consequence of the trauma of what they had to endure as well as demonic transfer from the abuser.

Rape

Rape is on the increase with many cases not even being reported because of the false guilt and shame the victims often feel about what has happened. Normally we think of rape being of women by men and that is still the most common form, but now, with the great rise in homosexual sin, men too can be raped.

Rape, sexual abuse and murder date back to the very earliest of Old Testament times. Genesis chapter 19 describes how the men of Sodom and Gomorrah attempted to force down the door of Lot's house so that they could have sex with Lot's male visitors. Genesis chapter 34 tells the story of how Shechem raped Dinah, which so infuriated her brothers that they avenged it by murder. Deuteronomy chapter 22 gives advice about dealing with men who commit rape. In some circumstances they were to be put to death and other times forced to marry the victim. Judges chapter 19 records the story of some evil men who demanded to have sex with a Levite but were offered his concubine. They gang-raped her and she was found dead in the morning.

It is a terrifying ordeal to be held down for enforced sex. The trauma and shock to the human spirit will need major healing. It will affect the victim in their body, soul and spirit and there will be an ungodly soul-tie established with the rapist that will also need to be broken. As people have shared their life stories with me, I have found that some individuals who have been abused or raped as children, find themselves continually victims to rape in later life.

I feel it is necessary to give a warning to young people who go to bars and discos. There is an appalling use of drugs to paralyze victims so that they are more vulnerable to sexual attack. A common drug used is Rohypnol, which can be put into the drink of an intended victim. Young people should be advised never to leave their drinks unattended. This form of rape is on the increase and can be totally devastating, and of course sexually transmitted diseases can also result.

The consequence of rape can be a victim spirit

I was involved in long-term ministry to a young woman and it seemed that wherever she went she was raped. Finally she left the UK, where she had been raped four times in different cities, for Australia. Within a month she had been raped there too. When she returned for yet more prayer ministry, she said: "It's as if I have a sign on my forehead which says, 'Rape me!' " We then sensed that, as a result of abuse, there was a negative spiritual deposit in her, like one half of a magnet, whose job function was to draw the spirit of the abuser. Wherever she went, this spirit spiritually attracted the spirit of the rapist, just like two halves of a magnet coming together.

We prayed into this, putting the cross of Jesus between her and any ruling spirit of abuse. We addressed the spirit of the abuser and asked Jesus to break all the ungodly soul-ties between her and the rapists. We separated out the spirit of the victim in her from the spirit of the abuser and put the cross and the blood between them. We cancelled, in Jesus' name, the power of this victim spirit whose job function was to draw to her the spirit of the abuser and commanded it to leave. Thankfully she was set free from the victim spirit and has not been raped since the prayer ministry.

Child abuse (pedophilia)

Child sexual abuse may occur within a family and be carried out by parents, grandparents, aunts, uncles, brothers or sisters. Abuse may start with inappropriate flirting or wrongful touching and progress eventually to penetrative sexual intimacy. The abuser will employ various threats to instill fear in the victim and keep the abuse secret. In this way many members of the same family may be victims of the abuser but this fact is often unknown to each other. Abusers receive self-gratification through their actions and will justify this by believing that there are no serious consequences for the victims or that they are initiating them into something pleasurable.

At Ellel Ministries we often minister to the sexually abused, who need much inner healing. I believe God hates child sexual abuse. Not all of it is incestuous or within the family but sometimes with known or trusted people who abuse the trust placed in them. Demonic spirits from the abuser can pass down the ungodly soul-tie, which is established through abuse. Not everyone who is abused goes on to abuse others but very few abusers have not at some time been victims of abuse themselves.

The perpetrators of sexual abuse will be controlled by demons and have major inner healing issues in their own life. They will invariably be experts at rationalizing or minimizing the consequences of their actions and may even portray themselves as the victim.

Because an abuser is demonized, simply punishing or sending him to prison is not going to bring change. At the end of the prison sentence the demon that needs to use the body of the abuser, in order to fulfill its demonic appetites, will simply rise up and this will mean that the person will most likely re-offend. Without deliverance ministry the abuser will continually struggle with temptation and incitement to abuse and never come into total freedom.

An abuser may hang around children's parks, schools, swimming pools and play areas. Parents can no longer send their children "out to play" and know that they will be safe. These men will often try to win the trust of the child and lure them into their vehicles, either to abuse them there or to take them to another location. In recent years there has been great concern about abusers attempting to "groom" victims through Internet chat rooms.

Ministering to an abuser

Sexual abusers will need to undergo the full penalty of the law for their offences. If this has already taken place and they are trying to seek ministry for healing and restoration they will need to prove that their salvation in Jesus and repentance of sin are real. They must have a clear understanding of the pain and harm they have caused their victims as well as acknowledging the harm and damage that they have caused themselves.

The abuser needs to be willing to be personally accountable to other Christians who would take on the role of discipling and mentoring. This should be established long before any deep-level prayer ministry is undertaken. I think the Christian discipleship process will need a team of caring people. The Christian counselors involved would need to be in good communication with doctors, psychiatrists, social workers and probation officers.

When a person has been a sexual abuser in the past extreme caution should be taken in exposing him to a position where he could be open to such temptation again in the future. Sadly the Church has been naïve in this respect, as demonstrated in the major issues which have had to be addressed in some established church organizations. Church-run children's homes today are no longer seen as a "safe haven" and anyone working with children now expects to have their records checked by police.

Healing for the victims

I am aware that many of you reading this book may yourselves have been victim of some form of abuse that has had a devastating impact on your life. Victims of abuse will always need healing in their lives. They will need to express the pain and anger about what has happened to them. They will need to regain a true sense of their identity and their value in the sight of God. They will almost certainly need some form of deliverance.

One of the most difficult steps in their healing will be to forgive all those who have abused them and those who should have protected them from this abuse. This is not easy to do but the innocent victim who prayed, *"Father, forgive them, for they do not know what they are doing"* for those who had abused Him and nailed Him on a cross, can help you if you ask Him. If you have been the victim of abuse you might like to pray this prayer:

> *Lord Jesus, You know everything about me. You know all about my rejection and abuse and the struggles I have with all my feelings about what happened and those that abused me. Help me to get to that place where I can be willing to forgive those who have damaged me and caused me pain. Help me to let go of all my bitterness and desire for revenge. Help me to be free of the past and move into the future You have for me. Amen.*

Turning the Final Page

In this book we have considered together many different aspects of sex and sexuality. I believe passionately that God's truth is for our very best, for our happiness, our health and our blessing. Jesus is holy and He calls His followers, His disciples, to be holy and blameless.

God has always wanted a holy people and He has not changed. As we read the Old Testament we see that the children of Israel were told not to intermarry with the nations round about them. This was because those nations worshiped false gods and idols and God knew if they intermarried they would be doing the same before long. All the way through their history they were disobedient.

We discover from 1 Kings 11:3 that Solomon, who had 700 wives of royal birth and 300 concubines, was led astray by his wives. He had a real problem with women! Verse 4 says:

> As Solomon grew old, his wives turned his heart after other gods, and his heart was not fully devoted to the LORD his God . . .

Verse 9 tells us:

> The LORD became angry with Solomon because his heart had turned away from the LORD . . .

Solomon did not keep the Lord's commands.

The area of sexuality is extremely important because seduction and succumbing to sexual temptation is so easy. If we follow the desires of the carnal nature in the area of our sexuality we quickly lose our heart and passion for the things of God.

Consequences of sexual sin

There are consequences of sexual sin. These can be physical as well as emotional, psychological and spiritual. For Solomon one of the consequences was the splitting and loss of the kingdom. Ungodly choices and sin choices always have ungodly consequences – the spiritual law of sowing and reaping will come into force:

> *Do not be deceived: God cannot be mocked. A man reaps what he sows. The one who sows to please his sinful nature, from that nature will reap destruction; the one who sows to please the Spirit, from the Spirit will reap eternal life.*
>
> (Galatians 6:7–8)

The apostle Paul reminds us:

> *But among you there must not be even a hint of sexual immorality, or of any kind of impurity, or of greed, because these are improper for God's holy people. Nor should there be obscenity, foolish talk or coarse joking, which are out of place, but rather thanksgiving. For of this you can be sure: No immoral, impure or greedy person – such a man is an idolater – has any inheritance in the kingdom of Christ and of God. Let no one deceive you with empty words, for because of such things God's wrath comes on those who are disobedient. Therefore do not be partners with them.*
>
> (Ephesians 5:3–7)

Sexual emotions and desires are very powerful.

*fter desire has conceived, it gives birth to sin; and sin,
is full-grown, gives birth to death.*

(James 1:15)

Our emotions and desires need to be under the Lordship of
Jesus Christ or control will be lost. Sexual sin is pleasurable and
used by the enemy as a believer's downfall. In the hymn "Love
Divine, All Loves Excelling"[1] there is a famous line which says,
"take away the love of sinning; Alpha and Omega be."

There is a huge price tag on sexual sin. Lust says, "I want it
now regardless of the consequences." Love waits – Jacob
worked seven years for Rachel. Sin separates us from God
because He is holy and cannot look at sin:

*If I regard iniquity in my heart,
The Lord will not hear.*

(Psalm 66:18 NKJV)

Some people are very good at claiming mitigating circumstances for sin – to justify it. They say such things as "God
knows I need to have this affair!" The enemy always agrees
when sin is entered into and adds his lies giving a false sense of
security, leading to the deception that sin is justified. Then
there are those who know it is sin and want the forgiveness of
God but don't want to "give up" the sin.

Emotional disturbance

Another consequence of sexual sin is emotional disturbance and
conflict. There can be self-destructive behavior. Wrongful
relationships often involve confrontation between the godly
and the ungodly. The whole of the spiritual life and relationship
with God can now be in a mess. Amazingly, Christians often try
to compartmentalize their sexual sin from their Christianity.
That means they can continue to go through the forms and the
practice of their faith as if nothing is wrong, taking communion
in church every Sunday, taking part as usual in the cell group

and audibly praying as if everything is "above board." Then in a separate compartment is sexual sin, as if the two don't affect each other. This is a gross deception.

More than for almost any other sin guilt, condemnation and shame are attached to sexual sin. By deeply repressing the guilt into a separate compartment, even though there is knowledge of the wrong and the involvement may be extensive, the sinner is able to lead a "double life."

A person can have a personality change as a result of living the double life, becoming edgy, nervous and jumpy over being "found out" and not allowing anyone to get close in case they discover the sin. Working hard to cover tracks, usually many lies have been told.

Other consequences of sexual sin

Sexual sins seldom come alone; lies and deception are close at hand together possibly with domination, control and manipulation. There is also the establishment of ungodly soul-ties with either a person or persons or the spirits behind such things as pornography.

Through sexual sin demonic rights will be given and there will be a need to address and receive deliverance from unclean spirits such as spirits of lust, promiscuity, seductive spirits and adulterous spirits. As a consequence of sexual abuse rights will be given to a victim spirit and spirits of abuse. Spirits of idolatry and self-idolatry are associated with such things as addictive masturbation.

There are now ever-increasing physical consequences of sexual sin in sexually transmitted diseases such as chlamydia, herpes, genital warts, HIV and AIDS.

Healing for the emotional damage in your life

Our Adamic nature or carnal flesh that has been damaged by the Fall, produces broken relationships, first with God and then others. Deep emotional damage and wounding through that separation follows. There is only one remedy and that is found in a covenant relationship with God the Father through Jesus Christ His Son by the power of the Holy Spirit.

God intended that our parents would image God to us and would provide the grounding we would need to relate to Him and others. Many of us sustain deep emotional damage and wounding because of lack of mother love and no nurture or affirmation from our father. None of this is our fault and therefore does not need to be repented of. It is what usually happens next which is the problem. It is how we tend to handle our deep damage and wounding on the inside, which is not just emotional but affects our core person – our human spirit. Our carnal nature or flesh rises up and says, "If no one will provide for this need, then I will survive by myself."

We think the love we long for is never coming so we turn to something else – that something else very often is sex. Our true, valid love needs can quickly turn into deformed perversions. There is so much tension on the inside: we feel disconnected, desperate for connection, and oppressed by tormenting spirits.

Soulish behaviors such as masturbation bring false hope and false comfort – a dead end. These hopes have to die before healing can begin. Nobody has the power to do this alone. Psychiatrists and therapists may help a little with the symptoms on a human level but only Jesus can make us completely whole on the inside. Healing has to happen to spirit, soul and body. The effects of the Fall can only be remedied by the death of the second Adam on the cross: *"by his wounds we are healed"* (Isaiah 53:5). Jesus said He came to heal the broken hearted (Isaiah 61:1) and actually no one can heal a broken heart except Jesus.

Deeply broken and emotionally damaged people can become sex addicts and be ensnared by sexual bondages that seem impossible to break. If you are asking God to heal the emotional damage in your life, you have to give up ever finding hope in these ungodly behaviors. There will never be enough sex, pornography, food, alcohol or drugs to fill the aching void that may reach right back to your conception, birth and formative development. You have to give up attempting to meet your true and valid needs for love with these counterfeit comforts.

To be truly healed, you will have to get in touch with the original pain. It is not necessary to re-live the memory but you will need to allow Jesus to bring the pain to the surface as well as any fear, anger and rejection. This could come in a progressive awareness of the roots of pain or it could all come to the surface very suddenly. As you get in touch with the depth of the pain, you will need to bring it to the cross. This is the point where, in union with Christ and His cross, you recognize that Jesus has borne every aspect of our fallen nature. Then open yourself up to the light of Christ and allow Jesus in, to deal with the root pain, and to bring healing. As we receive Christ's healing in this way, we will be

> *rooted and built up in him, strengthened in the faith as you were taught, and overflowing with thankfulness.*
>
> (Colossians 2:7)

Jesus has died our death, physically, emotionally, mentally and spiritually, on our behalf. He experienced rejection, abuse and isolation on our behalf. On the cross He cried out, *"My God, my God, why have you forsaken me?"* (Matthew 27:46; Mark 15:34). The Creator identifies Himself with the suffering of His created beings. The message of the cross has to reach all the unhealed areas of our lives. Ask Jesus to go to that wounded part so that the everlasting love of God is deeply communicated into the human spirit.

Silently wait upon God, who said: "I am *El Shaddai.*" [2] God the Father created us in families to receive love and nurture. He is the only one who can heal the deprivation in the human heart and spirit that is caused when parents are unable to provide it adequately. Allowing Jesus to bring a deep, lasting work of healing is like a dependent child looking up at Daddy with a trusting heart. Child-like worship comes from deep within the heart.

The message of true hope for those in sexual bondage, rooted in deep anxiety and an overwhelming sense of isolation, aloneness or deep abandonment from their past, is:

- God has never left you
- God will never abandon you
- God is always at work in you.

He who began a good work in you will surely finish it!

He knows that you may be too weakened by the damage and wounding to be able to do this for yourself. Lift your eyes up to Him. Stand in your adult self and allow God to go to that place deep inside, where you desperately need His healing flow.

Pray something like this:

> *Lord Jesus, I acknowledge my deep need of You. I choose to forgive all those who have hurt or neglected me. I forgive my mother for the deprivation that I have experienced, her lack of love and for her failure to meet my true needs. Please come and fill the center of my being.*
>
> *Please go to those places that I have tried to hide away. I invite You now to enter into those places where You know I desperately need Your love and Your healing. Lord, would You only allow those things to surface that I can handle and that You can control.*
>
> *I thank You, Jesus, for Your cross and I want to appropriate my healing that You won for me there. Come, Lord, to me now. I know that You delight to hear my cry. Forgive me for my wrong sexual behavior. Forgive me for trying to meet my deep unmet needs my way. Forgive me for trying to fill this void with defensive and compulsive behaviors.*
>
> *Lord, You have called me into being and chosen me to belong to You. Help me to come into a full and open*

relationship with You and to ask You to meet all my needs for love and affirmation. Please help me to place godly boundaries in my life. Restore to me a solid sense of being and a true identity in You alone. In Jesus' precious name. Amen.

How to get free from the bondage of sexual sin

Therefore confess your sins to each other and pray for each other so that you may be healed. The prayer of a righteous man is powerful and effective.

(James 5:16)

If sexual sin is an area of defeat in your life, own up. Tell God you recognize that it is sin. Try and find a trusted person that you can tell the exact nature of the sin to without hiding anything. This could be your husband/wife. Then work through the following steps:

- **Admit** that you have been powerless up to now with this sexual sin and that you need help to get free.
- **Agree** with God that He wants you to be a holy man or woman of God and that He can bring you into healing and wholeness of spirit, soul and body.
- **Repent**: turn from your sin. Decide that this sin is no longer going to be part of your life. Take on personal responsibility and accountability. Say sorry to God: "I am sorry – I was wrong – please forgive me and cleanse me."
- **Receive** the forgiveness of God for yourself.
- **Forgive** all others who got you involved in this sin. Forgive yourself – without forgiveness, healing cannot happen.
- **Change your beliefs**: deal with the lies of the enemy, and ask God to give you revelation of His truth. Change your thinking, "I can be free." Change your behavior and start to hate the thing that messes you up. The redeemed will is free to make godly choices – we are not victims.

- **Know** the things that trigger your ungodly sexual behavior and decide to avoid them. For example, if sexual sin is preceded by alcohol, then avoid alcohol. Because demons feed on soul power, after repentance, sexual spirits will need to be addressed and sent packing.

With the psalmist we can declare:

> *My flesh and my heart may fail*
> *but God is the strength of my heart*
> *and my portion forever!*

(Psalm 73:26)

How to walk in purity and keep free from sexual sin

The key to walking in purity is to have a passion for Jesus: search for a deeper, more intimate personal relationship with Him. Come into a radical experience of the powerful love that Father God has for only you. Recognize that all your God-given needs for security, significance and self-worth can be met in Jesus alone. Know who you are in Christ Jesus. You are clothed in the robe of Jesus' righteousness and you are dearly loved and special to Him.

Choose to be holy and blameless from now on. The enemy and your carnal nature will try to stop you but be encouraged that with God's help you can be an overcomer. The redeemed will is free to choose. Remember:

> *No temptation has seized you except what is common to man.*
> *And God is faithful; he will not let you be tempted beyond what*
> *you can bear. But when you are tempted, he will also provide a*
> *way out so that you can stand up under it.*

(1 Corinthians 10:13)

I recommend that you pray this prayer and keep a copy in your Bible to pray regularly:

> *Father, I come in Jesus' name and acknowledge my sexual sin* _____ (be specific). *I have sinned with my body, my mind and spirit and by doing so I have sinned against You. Your Word says that if I confess my sin You are faithful and just to forgive my sin and cleanse me from all unrighteousness. I ask You now, Lord Jesus, to forgive me and cleanse me from all the guilt, shame and uncleanness of my sin. Let Your living water flow over my soul so that I can feel clean on the inside.*
>
> *From this day onward I choose to walk in holiness and purity and to make You Lord of my sexuality and all its expression. In the power of Your Holy Spirit I choose to live in obedience to Your Holy Word in this and every area of my life.*
>
> *I declare that it is my desire to walk with integrity in all dealings with the opposite sex and that with God's help I will keep my heart clean. Help me, Lord, to live a life of purity in the area of my sexuality.*
>
> *In Jesus' mighty name, Amen.*

Men and women are made in the image of God and intended by God to portray His heart to the world. The deepest needs of the human heart are met in knowing God the Father through Jesus; in knowing Him passionately, tenderly and vulnerably. He alone can fill our empty love tanks, so that having received the fullness of His everlasting covenantal love, shed abroad in our hearts, we will then, and only then, be qualified to enter into horizontal relationship with others.

The greatest human relationships are marriage and true friendship. We can give of ourselves into these only when we have received the fullness of God's love for us. We can then worship Him in return and know that He is loving and kind towards all that He has made.

The driving force behind the ungodly expression of our sexuality is a seeking after false love and acceptance. To walk into purity and holiness we need to know more of His love in our lives. He is the only one who will never let us down.

**Come alive, be healed, and know
that God loves you personally.**

Notes

1. Charles Wesley (1707–88).
2. *El Shaddai* means "I am God Almighty"; cf. Genesis 17:1.

APPENDIX

Frequently Asked Questions about Contraception

As I teach on the subject of sex and sexuality I am often asked questions relating to family planning and contraception, some of which I include here. My answers have been developed in consultation with a medical doctor who is a member of the Ellel team.

Should Christians use contraception?

The decision whether or not to use contraception is a personal issue for each couple to consider prayerfully. There will often be a number of considerations that need to be thought through and over the centuries Christians have come to different conclusions.

God has certainly given us the gift of sex and intended us to celebrate and enjoy it. However, there is no getting round the fact that for most couples this is simply not possible without contraception. Otherwise we would still be seeing families with ten to fifteen children! In centuries gone by, this was sometimes necessary as the infant death rate was high, survival was a struggle and life expectancy was short.

However, times have changed and in the twenty-first century modern medicine has made dramatic advances in curing disease, reducing infant mortality and increasing life expectancy. But it's not all good news, for those very advances are now bringing their own problems ... Population explosion! At the time of writing the world population is still increasing by 1 million people every five days.[1] At the present growth rate the world population will double in the next fifty-three years. That's a lot of extra people! Even in the UK we can expect an extra 7 million people over the next fifty years. It will not be long before we will run into the serious problems of over-crowding, bringing with it increasing demands in the face of dwindling resources.

Contraception not only provides one method of tackling this problem, it also allows couples to enjoy sexual fulfillment, while still being able to plan their children, within their financial and emotional constraints.

Of course, before marriage, I would advise and, indeed, urge abstinence as the only way forward. God gave us these instructions as He knew what was good for us! The world has ignored God's instructions at its peril and, sadly, often Christians have too. We now pay the price of unwanted pregnancies, increasing abortions, sexually transmitted diseases, broken relationships and emotional and spiritual scars.

At what point in the menstrual cycle is a woman fertile?

The menstrual cycle is the process in a woman in which an egg develops, is released, and the lining of the womb is prepared for any possible pregnancy. This lining is then shed, called menstruation or a "period," if a pregnancy does not occur.

The majority of women have a fairly regular menstrual cycle of twenty-eight to thirty days. However, it can vary from twenty-one to forty days and still be quite normal.

The first day of the period we call day one of the cycle. At around day twelve to sixteen a woman will produce an egg (ovulate) and therefore could become pregnant if she had sexual intercourse. An egg can only survive twelve to twenty-four hours once it has been released from the ovary. However, since sperm can survive up to seven days in the Fallopian tubes, an egg could be fertilized by a sperm ejaculated up to seven days previously.

Therefore, the fertile time is quite unpredictable in length and usually lasts several days, roughly from about day eight to sixteen. However, it can be much longer and women have been known to ovulate at almost any point in the cycle. If a woman has an irregular cycle, ovulation takes place roughly fourteen days before the next period, rather than after the last one.

How should you decide what contraception to use?

Each couple seeking contraception will need to look at their personal circumstances, age, social factors and health issues, as these will all influence their choice. This should be done in consultation with a doctor.

However, I believe that the most important question to ask is, "How does the method work?" Does it work before or after fertilization? In order to discover the reason why that question is so important, we need first to ask another crucial question, "When does life start?"

When does life start?

Is it at fertilization? Or implantation? Or sometime later?

From a physical point of view, conception usually takes place in the Fallopian tubes. This happens when an egg meets a sperm and the egg becomes fertilized. As soon as fertilization occurs, the egg starts dividing and producing new cells. The fertilized egg, now called an embryo, is swept down into the womb, where it implants about eight to ten days after fertilization. The placenta then forms, which helps provide nourishment for the embryo as it continues to grow into a fetus.

Most Christians believe that life starts either at fertilization or implantation. Personally, I would suggest that life begins at fertilization. This is the point when the new life first begins and the cells start dividing and growing. At implantation, the growing embryo merely swaps its energy source from the on-board supply in the egg to the "plugged-in" supply of the placenta – like swapping from battery to mains power on your laptop! However, the process of dividing and growing has already started and continues unabated.

In the Psalms, David talks about God seeing him in the womb, clearly expressing his belief that his life had begun before birth:

> *you knit me together in my mother's womb...*
> *My frame was not hidden from you*
>   *when I was made in the secret place...*
>   *your eyes saw my unformed body.*
>
> (Psalm 139:13, 15–16)

However, in Psalm 51 he goes one step further and says,

> *Surely I was sinful at birth,*
>   *sinful from the time my mother conceived me.*
>
> (v. 5)

Here he identifies his humanity and even his personal sinful nature even from the point of conception!

Finally, through our experience in prayer ministry and counseling, we find that damage in people's lives can even be traced back or revealed by God to have started at conception. For example, if someone was conceived in rape or abuse, we may find that the seeds of rejection or fear were planted at that point. We have seen numerous amazing examples of God healing such pain and trauma, and have little doubt that conception is one of the most significant moments in our lives!

Which forms of contraception are therefore advisable for Christians?

As I believe that life starts at conception, I would suggest that Christians need to choose a method of contraception that works before conception and therefore prevents the sperm and egg meeting at all. Contraceptives that work after conception prevent the fertilized egg from implanting in the womb, but by this stage life has already begun.

There is often some confusion about how exactly the hormonal methods work. This is because the *main* action of the Combined Pill, Cerazette, injections and implants is to prevent ovulation, but they also work by making the cervical mucus hostile to sperm penetration, as well as by preventing a fertilized egg from implanting. However, I have assigned them to the following groups based on the generally accepted *main* mode of action!

I have therefore divided contraceptives into two groups:

1. Contraception that works before conception (and is therefore OK to use)

(a) *"The Pill"* (also called the Combined Pill, COCP or Combined Oral Contraceptive Pill). This is a hormonal pill containing both estrogen and progesterone and is 99 per cent effective. It mainly works by preventing eggs being produced. It is usually taken for twenty-one days a month, followed by a seven-day pill-free interval, during which time the woman has a withdrawal bleed. It is usually a very good, reliable form of contraception, especially in young people, as long as it is taken properly. However, it does have side effects, which occasionally can be serious, including blood clots and strokes. Therefore it is not suitable for all women, especially those who are overweight, older, smokers if aged over thirty-five, suffer from migraine or a family history of blood clots. This type of contraceptive also comes in patch form.

(b) *Cerazette.* This is a new mini-pill and is also 99 per cent effective. It seems that although this is a mini-pill, it mainly works also by preventing ovulation.

(c) *Contraceptive injection.* This contains a progesterone hormone and is given every eight to twelve weeks, depending on the injection. It is over 99 per cent effective and works by preventing ovulation and changing cervical mucus.

(d) *Implant.* This is a small plastic rod that is placed just under the skin in the upper arm and releases progesterone. It is over 99 per cent effective and works for up to three years without needing to be changed. It works by preventing ovulation, as well as by changing cervical mucus. The implant currently available in the UK is called Implanon.

(e) *Barrier methods*:
   - *Condoms.* These are readily available and easily used, but not very reliable as they can split or slip off, and are difficult to always use well. They can be 98 per cent effective if used correctly.
   - *Diaphragm.* This is a rubber cap inserted into the vagina by the woman before intercourse. Spermicidal cream is often used in conjunction with a diaphragm. However, it is not very reliable, especially in younger, more fertile women. It is 92–96 per cent effective.

(f) *Irreversible methods*:
   - *Vasectomy.* This is where the man's spermatic cord is cut. It is performed under local anesthetic and is simple to do. It can take 2–3 months after the operation before all the sperm have cleared from the semen.
   - *Female sterilization.* This requires a general anesthetic and therefore carries more risk than a vasectomy.
   In this operation the Fallopian tubes are cut and tied. Both these methods must be considered to be irreversible. Although it is sometimes possible to try to reverse them,

there is no guarantee that it will be successful and is often expensive to do.

(g) *Natural methods.* This means using fertility indicators which monitor when a woman is fertile and avoiding sexual intercourse during that period or using the withdrawal method, or *coitus interruptus.* There are several ways of monitoring fertility, including monitoring for a change in temperature or a change in mucus around ovulation, and using a kit called "Persona." These methods are only 94 per cent effective.

2. After conception
(and therefore not usually recommended)

(a) *Coil or IUCD (Intra-Uterine Contraceptive Device).* This is usually a T-shaped plastic or copper device and is inserted into the womb by a family doctor. It is cheap and relatively easy to fit and only needs to be changed every five years, resulting in it being frequently used all over the world. It works by preventing a fertilized egg from implanting in the womb. Instead the embryo is shed like a heavy period.

The Mirena coil is similar in shape to the normal coil but contains progesterone within it. This also works on the cervical mucus, stops embryos from implanting and may also work by preventing ovulation, but this cannot be guaranteed.

(b) *Mini Pill or POP (Progesterone Only Pill).* This includes all Mini Pills except Cerazette. These are slightly less effective than the Combined Pill and work by changing the cervical mucus, as well as stopping a fertilized egg from implanting. The only situation where it is possibly adequate from a Christian point of view is when a woman is totally breast-feeding a baby, and not giving any formula top-up feeds. In this situation she will have the added natural contraception that comes from 100 per cent

breast-feeding. The Combined Pill is contra-indicated
while breast-feeding.

(c) *Morning-after Pill.* This is a hormonal pill which is taken
up to three days after unprotected sexual intercourse and
works by preventing a fertilized egg from implanting in
the womb. The sooner it is taken, the more effective it
is, but even then it is not always effective.

Where can I get up-to-date advice?

Contraception is a slippery animal to handle! Modern, safe,
cheap contraception is a relatively new phenomenon and is
even now still evolving and changing. You can get to the point
of finally having an understanding of the options, but then they
slip through your fingers again, as they change so frequently.
Even doctors find it hard to keep up with all the changes!

The information given above is accurate in the year 2006, but
in a year or two's time there will no doubt be yet more available
options.

I would always advise you to seek up-to-date expert medical
advice from your family doctor. In the UK, advice is also
available from the Family Planning Association (fpa). It produces excellent leaflets for patients, available from general
practitioners, via its UK helpline (0845 310 1334) or via its
website (www.fpa.org.uk). The Christian Medical Fellowship
in the UK also provide excellent information on contraception
and a number of other medico-ethical issues, both in their
literature and on their website: www.cmf.org.uk.

Note _____

1. Information acquired from the Population Reference Bureau
   (www.prb.org).

About Ellel Ministries

Our Vision

Ellel Ministries is a non-denominational Christian Mission Organization with a vision to resource and equip the Church by welcoming people, teaching them about the Kingdom of God and healing those in need (Luke 9:11).

Our Mission

Our mission is to fulfill the above vision throughout the world, as God opens the doors, in accordance with the Great Commission of Jesus and the calling of the Church to proclaim the Kingdom of God by preaching the good news, healing the broken-hearted and setting the captives free. We are, therefore, committed to evangelism, healing, deliverance, discipleship and training. The particular scriptures on which our mission is founded are Isaiah 61:1–7; Matthew 28:18–20; Luke 9:1–2; 9:11; Ephesians 4:12; 2 Timothy 2:2.

Our Basis of Faith

God is a Trinity. God the Father loves all people. God the Son, Jesus Christ, is Savior and Healer, Lord and King. God the Holy Spirit indwells Christians and imparts the dynamic power by which they are enabled to continue Christ's ministry. The Bible is the divinely inspired authority in matters of faith, doctrine and conduct, and is the basis for teaching.

For more information

Please visit our website at www.ellelministries.org for full up-to-date information about the world-wide work of Ellel Ministries.

Ellel Ministries Centers

International Head Office

Ellel Grange

Ellel, Lancaster LA2 0HN, UK
t: +44 (0) 1524 751651
f: +44 (0) 1524 751738
e: info.grange@ellelministries.org

Ellel Glyndley Manor

Stone Cross, Pevensey, E. Sussex
BN24 5BS, UK
t: +44 (0) 1323 440440
f: +44 (0) 1323 440877
e: info.glyndley@ellelministries.org

Ellel Pierrepont

Frensham, Farnham, Surrey
GU10 3DL, UK
t: +44 (0) 1252 794060
f: +44 (0) 1252 794039
e: info.pierrepont@ellelministries.org

Ellel Scotland

Blairmore House, Glass, Huntly,
Aberdeenshire AB54 4XH, Scotland
t: +44 (0) 1466 799102
f: +44 (0) 1466 700205
e: info.scotland@ellelministries.org

Ellel Ministries Ireland

35 Beanstown Road, Lisburn, County Antrim,
BT28 3QS, Northern Ireland
t: +44 (0) 28 9260 7162
e: info.northernireland@ellelministries.org

Ellel Ministries Africa

PO Box 39569, Faerie Glen 0043, Pretoria,
South Africa
t: +27 (0) 12 809 0031/1172
f: +27 12 809 1173
e: info.africa@ellelministries.org

Ellel Ministries Australia (Sydney)

Gilbulla, 710 Moreton Park Road, Menangle,
2568, NSW, Australia
t: +61 (02) 4633 8102
f: +61 (02) 4633 8201
e: info.gilbulla@ellelministries.org

Ellel Ministries Australia Headquarters (Perth)
Springhill, PO Box 609, Northam, WA, 6401, Australia
t: +61 (08) 9622 5568
f: +61 (08) 9622 5123
e: info.springhill@ellelministries.org

Ellel Ministries Canada Derbyshire Downs
183 Hanna Rd., RR#2, Westport, Ontario, K0G 1X0, Canada
t: +1 (613) 273 8700
e: info.ontario@ellelministries.org

Ellel Ministries Canada West
10-5918 5 St SE, Calgary, Alberta, T2H 1L4, Canada
t: +1 (403) 238 2008
f: +1 (866) 246 5918
e: info.calgary@ellelministries.org

Ellel Ministries France (Fraternité Chrétienne)
10 Avenue Jules Ferry, 38380 Saint Laurent du Pont, France
t: +33 (0) 476 554 266
e: info.france@ellelministries.org

Ellel Ministries Germany
Bahnhoffstr. 43-47, 72213 Altensteig, Deutschland
w: www.ellelgermany.de
t: +49 (0) 7453 275 51
e: info.germany@ellelministries.org

Ellel Ministries Hungary
Veresegyház, PF17, 2112, Hungary
t/f: +36 28 362396
e: info.hungary@ellelministries.org

Ellel Central & Eastern Europe Development
Veresegyház, PF17, 2112, Hungary
t: +36 28 362410 / f: +36 28 362396
e: info.regionalnations@ellelministries.org

Ellel India
502, Orchid, Holy Cross Road, IC Colony, Borivli West, Mumbai 400 103, India
mobile: +91 (0) 93 2224 5209
e: info.india@ellelministries.org

Ellel Ministries Malaysia
Lot 2, Ground and 1st Floor, Wisma Leven Lorong Margosa 2, Luyang Phase 8, 88300 Kota Kinabalu, Sabah, Malaysia
t: +6088 270246
f: +6088 270280
e: info.malaysia@ellelministries.org

Ellel Ministries Netherlands
Wichmondseweg 19, 7223 LH Baak, Netherlands
t: +31 575 441452
e: info.netherlands@ellelministries.org

Ellel Ministries New Zealand
info.newzealand@ellelministries.org

Ellel Ministries Norway
Stiftelsen Ellel Ministries Norge, Hogstveien 2, 2006 Løvenstad, Norge (Norway)
t: +47 67413150
e: info.norway@ellelministries.org

Ellel Ministries Singapore
Thomson Post Office, PO Box 204, Singapore 915707
t: +65 6252 4234
f: +65 6252 3792
e: info.singapore@ellelministries.org

Ellel Ministries Sweden
Kvarnbackavägen 4 B, 711 92 Vedevåg, Sweden
t: +46 581 93140
e: info.sweden@ellelministries.org

Ellel Ministries USA
1708 English Acres Drive, Lithia, Florida, 33547, USA
t: +1 (813) 737 4848
f: +1 (813) 737 9051
e: info.usa@ellelministries.org

*All details are correct at time of going to press (November 2012) but are subject to change.

CPSIA information can be obtained
at www.ICGtesting.com
Printed in the USA
FFOW03n0248080515
13185FF